SIDDHA MARG

VOLUME 2

Mahamandaleshwar Swami Nityananda

ISBN 978-1-7363942-2-9

Shanti Mandir
51 Muktananda Marg
Walden, NY 12586, U.S.A.

Tel: +1 (845) 778–1008
www.shantimandir.com

The eternal teachings...

Issues 19 through 44 of the magazine *Siddha Marg* are compiled in this volume. The purpose of *Siddha Marg* is to share the eternal teachings, or *sanātan dharma*. Formal talks, study, conversations, questions and answers, kirtan, meditation, and silence are some of the methods used by Gurudev, Mahāmandaleshwar Swami Nityānanda Saraswatī, to share his ruminations on and expression of the universal philosophy.

TABLE OF CONTENTS

Become Empty 1
The City of Nine Gates 5
Baba Knew 9
The Eight Limbs of Yoga 13
The Yamas 19
Immersed in the Mantra 25
I Am Not the Body 35
Knowledge Comes from Within 39
The Best Is to Be Quiet 43
Equal Vision 49
Compassion, Forgiveness, Straightforwardness 53
How Do I Become Free? 59
Live the Truth 63
Don't Become the Soap 67
The State of Indifference 71
Ritual Is a Part of Life 77
Where the Goddess Dwells 83
You Are Not Alone 89
Salutations to the Goddess 93
What Are You Going to Offer? 97
The World Is as You See It 101
Where Did You Put Your Umbrella? 105
The Mind's True Nature 109
Down the Chimney 113
Be That Drop of Honey 117
The Veil of Illusion 123
The Day of the Guru 127
May I Never Forget You 131
From Darkness to Light 135
You Are Blessed 143
The Outlook of Śiva 147
I Am That 151
A Natural Practice 155
Responsibility 159
Cooperation 163
Adaptability 167

The River Doesn't Drink Its Own Water 171
Give What You Want to Get. 175
Ripen as You Age. 179
Three Qualities of Giving 183
Become Steady. 187
Become Holy 191
Which Is Real?. 193
Baba's Message 199
Rewind the Tape of Life. 203
Soft as Butter 207
The Salt Doll 211
Not the Doer. 215
Discipline and Dedication 219
The Four Means 223
The Sixty Qualities 227
There Is Nothing That Is Not Consciousness. 235
Glossary 237

BECOME EMPTY

Namaste. Good morning. Gidday. With great respect and love I'd like to welcome everyone here to *satsaṅg*.

The *Bhagavad Gītā* says, "If you are born, it is certain that you will die. And if you die, it is certain that you will be reborn."

There is no way of avoiding this. I'm sure many of us, with our doctors and our insurance policies, would like to live forever. And we do our best. But the sages and scriptures tell us that on the day that it is destined, we will go.

In *Play of Consciousness*, Baba Muktānanda says, "I have seen death with my own eyes."

We know he was not talking about his physical death because he was still alive at the time. He meant the death of the ego.

I thought we should begin there. For most spiritual seekers, the greatest obstacle is their ego. As one progresses in understanding, in wisdom, the ego gets subtler. Therefore, it becomes even more difficult to let go. One thinks, "I don't have an ego because I have been meditating, I have been praying, I have been doing so many practices."

Baba used to tell a great story.

Nasruddin is a therapist. Somebody goes to him and says, "I get these headaches."

Nasruddin says, "Do you smoke?"

He says, "No."

"Do you drink?"

He says, "No."

Nasruddin asks him, "Do you do this? Do you do that?"

To everything, the man says, "No, no, no, no."

Nasruddin says, "I think I know the reason for your headache. Your sense of righteousness, of always being correct, of being proper and in the meanwhile looking down upon others, is the cause of your headaches."

Baba never advised us—and neither would I—to smoke and drink and do all these things. No. Just get off your high horse. Come to planet Earth and live amidst everybody else.

Understand and know your Self.

The whole idea of separation, of duality, of the other, must die first. I didn't use the words "gotten rid of" or "eradicated" or "lost." It must die. To understand the death of any great saint, we must realize that his identity with "I" and "mine" is gone.

Bhagavān Nityānanda always referred to his body as "this one."

It would be a challenge for all of us in society to say, "This one wants chai." "This one would like lunch." "This one wants to go for a walk." Even when speaking to friends who are on the path with us, it doesn't come out as easily and naturally as "I want some chai."

You would have to train yourself to say "this one." If you did, then when you were in deep sleep and somebody woke you up, you would not even think, "Who woke me up?" or "Who is disturbing me?" You would simply think, "Who has woken this body up?"

Many years ago on a train, I found a riddle in a magazine. From a tree, a ripe mango is seen falling. One who did not see that mango goes running. The mango is picked up by a third one. Then the mango is eaten by someone else—not the one who's seen it, not the one who's run, not the one who's picked it up.

The question is "Who are these four?"

All the parts of the "somebody" are parts of the body: the eyes see the mango, the legs run, the hand picks it up, the mouth eats it. Although they all live within the body, they act independently. We could even go a step further and say, "Who is actually the enjoyer?"

The death of the ego is a big subject. The singer Hari Om Sharan says, "O Lord, let my mind, which is filled with pride, touch the dust of Your feet. Let my mind, which is filled with ego and fluctuations, repeat the name of the Self." It's a poem we heard often around Baba. He says, "I have come to the faultless one, seeking refuge. My prayer is this: let me become empty and let the flame of love light up within me."

Become empty. Here is a very simple example. A professor goes to a Zen master and wants knowledge.

The Zen master offers him tea and begins to pour. When the cup is full, the tea flows into the saucer. The Zen master keeps pouring and the tea overflows onto the table.

When the tea begins to overflow onto the floor, the professor says, "Wait! Stop! You can see the cup is already full."

The Zen master says, "Ah. Your cup is also full. Just as the tea overflows onto the saucer and the table and the floor, the knowledge that will be given to you will pour out. It will not stay in you."

THE CITY OF NINE GATES

If you have ever walked up to a fruit tree and put your hand to a fruit that is ripe, it falls into your hand. You haven't twisted it or turned it or done anything but put your hand to it. I love it when that happens, because then I know the fruit is perfectly ripe. You eat it right then and there.

That is how ready one has to be for death.

We hope that we never die. Right? If I ask anyone in this room, "Do I want to go yet?"—the "yet" is not necessary, but we always add that "yet"—you would say, "No, I still have a few things I'd like to achieve, some things left to do." And fear comes up. Of course, maybe now you'd respond differently because you think, "I'm spiritually knowledgeable." But think about it and ask yourself this question when you are alone.

We hear that somebody is in a coma, and the person hangs on and on. I would say that shows the amount of attachment that individual has to the body. There is nothing else that can hold them besides attachment. A yogi is exactly the opposite. He says, "I'm ready," and when the time has come, he's gone.

The yogi simply sheds his body at the time of death.

The sages teach us, "Don't cry, don't be sad. It's only the external cover that is shed. The inner core is still alive and well. It is looking for the next body to enter."

In the eighth chapter of the *Bhagavad Gītā*, Kṛṣṇa explains that the body is known as the city of nine gates. At the time of death, the yogi withdraws all his senses. He closes all his gates, and he brings his *prāṇa*, the vital force, to the heart region. This is where the yogic scriptures say the mind dwells in this body.

According to the Indian tradition, the soul leaves this body in one of four main ways. One is through the anal opening. When people excrete as they leave their body, you have to assume that is the port they used. It is said that is the worst form of passing. The person needs to do more good, to live a better life. The soul has to uplift itself.

Another port is through the mouth. The mouth of such a person is open at the time of death. The next port is through the eyes. The port yogis use is this at the top of the head, what we call the *sahasrāra*.

As his vital force rises, the yogi repeats *Oṁ*.

Now, you have to realize that in this moment of death, one can only repeat *Oṁ* if one has been repeating *Oṁ* throughout one's life. It doesn't happen accidentally. Even if a CD or iPod is playing *Oṁ*—which many people do for a family member—it doesn't matter. Every cell, every molecule, in the body needs to be repeating *Oṁ*. If the yogi has prepared himself, as he repeats *Oṁ*, his soul, the *Ātman*, will exit through the sahasrāra.

As Kṛṣṇa says, that individual attains the highest. He has freed himself from the cycle of birth and death.

We told ourselves, "I'm going to the Somers retreat today." On Sunday, we'll say, "I'm going back to Melbourne." Whether you go by car or with a friend, everybody knows where you have gone. In the same way, the yogi tells his Ātman that his destination is what is expressed through *Oṁ*.

The *Upaniṣads* describe *Oṁ* as the primordial sound from which creation has come into being. Everything is contained within *Oṁ*. When you listen to pure sound and let go of all other variations, the yogis say, then you hear *Oṁ*.

Baba's teaching was "Remember God and remember death." He would say you never know when death will come, so if you remember God all the time, then you will remember God at the moment of death. This is the same teaching Kṛṣṇa gave: "Remember *Oṁ* as you are leaving the body."

You will only remember *Oṁ* if you have been chanting *Oṁ* all along. We do it three times before we begin a chant, and sometimes I think, "Maybe, after doing this for so many years, it's time to increase it to five. Or eleven."

BABA KNEW

Over the years, as I have traveled, I have met people who asked, "Do you think Baba knew?"

The answer then and now is yes. And I don't mean because he appointed me successor, and therefore it is clear he knew. But if you look at all the things he physically did and created for that day, October 2, 1982, you would say he knew that was his time to leave.

For sure, in May 1977, on his birthday, he got a good idea of how many more years he would live on this planet. After that day, the speed with which he worked was amazing.

I was there that day, that morning. He told his attendant to tell the doctor and his nurse to be in his room after lunch because he was going to have a big heart attack.

Of course, we didn't have lunch.

My job was to answer the door and manage who came in and out. Because, you know, when news spread throughout the ashram, everybody wanted to be by Baba. They felt they could be of help.

So Baba had lunch. Then he came and lay on his bed. He rang the bell and said, "Call the doctor."

Being young, one wondered, "How can he manipulate it to have a heart attack now?" But we were taught never to question him, to do what he said. So we did.

The doctors came. Everybody came. And then… he was gone.

Baba's bed was against the wall, and at the foot of the bed were a bunch of people. The word had gotten out, "He's gone."

Around 2:30 pm, Baba opened his eyes. He looked at everybody and said, "What are you doing? Have you had lunch?" The main doctor looked at him and said, "But, Baba, you were gone."

He said, "Well, I talked to my Guru. He sent me back."

Some months later he explained in great detail in a talk how he had left his body and his Guru had said, "Muktānanda, you have work to do. You can't leave yet."

My own belief—which I have never confirmed or discussed with anybody—is that his prārabdha karma as Swami Muktānanda finished on that day in May 1977. You can compare how he looked before and how he looked after. If you study his pictures with an open mind, you can see the change. He became younger.

As we traveled on the third tour, Baba was in touch with Venkappa, the manager of the ashram. Baba had one of the rooms where he had lived removed, and a pit dug there. Wood planks were put on top. When he came back from the world tour, in the evening when nobody was around, he went with Venkappa and checked that the work had been done. He saw that the place to bury him was ready. And he danced on those wooden planks.

We went to Kashmir in September. After we came back, Baba said to every person he met, "Come next Saturday. Come next Saturday. Come next Saturday."

Some people took him seriously and came. Others thought, "Baba just wants me to spend the weekend with him. I'll go like I always do, on Sunday." Of course, they said, "Yes, Baba I'm coming."

Life was normal in the ashram. At one point, the swami in charge of the kitchen came to Baba and said, "How many *laddus* should we prepare for Sunday?"

The 3rd of October was to be a *bhaṇḍārā*, and Baba said, "Five thousand."

The swami said, "But we are only a thousand."

Baba said, "Five thousand."

Of course Baba left his body on the 2nd, and so for the next three days, the ashram was open twenty-four hours a day. The news spread, and people from all over the world came for Baba's final *darśan*.

It is believed that a great saint who has become one with Consciousness, become one with Truth, carries that vibration within him. Therefore, the place where such great beings are buried is called a *samādhi* shrine. Their Consciousness radiates from that place and continues to bless those who visit it.

We buried Baba on the 5th of October. The 6th of October was my twentieth birthday. We had a thirty-day chant of *Oṁ Namo Bhagavāte Muktānandāya*. You could feel Baba's presence there just as much as it had always been. Even today hearing that chant takes me back to the feeling of October 1982.

One night, I had dream. In the dream, it was around ten o'clock in the morning. I was walking in the hallway outside what we knew as Bagve's office. I had come out of the temple and turned the corner, and Baba was coming toward me. It was just the two of us.

I said to him, "But, Baba, we buried you some days ago. You are supposed to be inside that samādhi."

He laughed. He said, "Now I am free of that body. I can go wherever I want. Nobody can tell me where I can go or cannot go."

The scriptures say that beings such as Bhagavān and Baba have a choice. They have the freedom to be born or not to be born. As long as you are bound by the cycle of karma, you will come, you will go, you will come, you will go. But a free being just comes, does what needs to be done, and goes.

Ādi Śaṅkarācārya lives on this planet for about thirty years. Swami Vivekānanda was barely forty when he passed.

Some people say, "Why do good people only live for so long?" I think they infuse goodness upon this earth, and then that goodness stays for a long time.

THE EIGHT LIMBS OF YOGA

This question refers to two things: the *yamas* and *niyamas*. But we will look at the whole package, which is *aṣṭāṅga* yoga, the eight limbs of yoga.

Recently I heard a story about a young man who goes to visit a swami. He says, "I want to learn to meditate."

The swami starts talking to him about *āsana*, *prāṇāyāma*, yama, niyama, *pratyāhāra*, and *dhāraṇā*, which are the six things that need to happen before you meditate.

The man says, "I only want to meditate. I don't want to know about āsana, prāṇāyāma, yama, niyama, pratyāhāra, and dhāraṇā. I just want to meditate."

Swamiji asks him, "Do you want to learn a partial yoga or do you want to learn the complete yoga? Do you want one little part or do you want the whole thing?"

The āsanas, or postures, you learn in hatha yoga are only one part of aṣṭāṅga yoga.

The yogis tell us that the process of yoga takes place like a child developing inside its mother's womb. All the limbs develop at the same time. The child doesn't develop the head, then the torso, then the legs and feet and arms. All the parts develop simultaneously.

In the same way, you can't say, "I'll just do āsana until I get good at it. Then I'll do prāṇāyāma. Then I'll do yama. Then I'll do niyama. Then I'll do pratyāhāra. Then I'll do dhāraṇā. Then I'll do *dhyāna*. And then I will get to samādhi."

All of these need to happen within the twenty-four-hour span of your life; that is, on a regular, daily basis. You have to do āsana. You have to do prāṇāyāma. You have to do yama. You have to do niyama. You have to do pratyāhāra. You have to do dhāraṇā. You have to do dhyāna. You have to do samādhi.

The first limb people learn about is āsana. In our society today, hatha yoga has been brought into the gym, and many people think that's all there is to yoga. But hatha yoga is not meant to be a complete yoga unto itself.

The word *hatha* comes from *ha* and *tha*, meaning the sun and moon, respectively. When you begin to do hatha yoga, you realize the effect it has upon you within. What happens to your physical body is only the by-product of what happens within you. You find that you have more muscle. You feel better. But the main change is what takes place within. Am I correct, yoga teachers?

Āsana means to be established in a particular position. Patañjali describes this in the *Yoga Sūtras* by saying, "Be steady, be still." In order to get into meditation, you have to first become steady, you have to become alert. You have to be in a place of *sukha*.

Sukha often is translated as pleasure, but I think of it as contentment. Unless you are content, you can't practice yoga. You can't sit because you are not still, you are not content.

As you begin the practice of hatha yoga, it takes some months to some years to understand what is actually taking place in your body. A yogi has to study for a period of years. Today, there are week-long courses and maybe even weekend courses. People take them and say, "Now I know hatha yoga." But if you go to such a person to learn hatha yoga, you won't learn hatha yoga. You will learn a few movements but not the full yoga.

After āsana, the next limb is prāṇāyāma, control of the breath. The physical postures and the movement of the breath have to be done together. Prāṇa—which we won't go into right now—refers to the life force, which performs five functions within the body. And *āyāma* means expansion. We allow the breath to become long, to expand.

Yoga philosophy teaches us that the quality of our prāṇa is related to the state of our mind.

When you are agitated, people tell you, "Take a deep breath." They want you to calm down by taking a deep breath. Prāṇāyāma involves learning to take full inhalations and full exhalations.

The question was about yamas and niyamas. We'll get into that. They are the third and fourth limbs.

The fifth limb is pratyāhāra. *Āhāra* is food, nourishment.

The *Bhagavad Gītā* explains pratyāhāra using the example of a tortoise. We have all seen how a tortoise withdraws into its shell. Similarly, a yogi learns to withdraw his senses. He does not nourish his senses or his mind with external objects. Rather, he takes nourishment from within himself.

For example, a child is crying. So—at least today—the parent immediately gives him an iPad or an iPhone or an ice cream or something. Over time, the child develops a habit of thinking "Whenever I am sad or upset or I am crying, my senses need to go out and grab something."

Forty or fifty years later, when the physical body has developed one or another sickness, the health-care practitioner tells the person to stay away from most of these things. Of course, society today has created other things that can satisfy the need to grab onto something external. But the yogi says no. Simply go inside. Practice pratyāhāra.

As you go inside, you need something to help you. So Patañjali introduces dhāraṇā. *Dha* means to hold, to focus the mind.

Think about how disturbed and agitated the mind can be. One of the first things a meditator notices is "my mind is running." If I say that it is running in a million different directions, that would not be an exaggeration.

The mind is not satisfied. It's not contented. It's not at peace. Therefore, the body is fidgety. Therefore, the breath is uneven. Therefore, thoughts are disturbed.

The sage says, "When you have done āsana, when you have done prāṇāyāma, when you have done yama, when you have done niyama, then you come to dhāraṇā."

Because the question today is about the yamas and niyamas, we will focus just upon that much.

Recently I read something I thought I'd share.

A modern sage says, "People who are withdrawing from excessive activity are not causing any damage either to themselves, the society, the world, the environment, or the planet. It is only people who are engaged in activity in absolute unawareness who are truly destroying this world."

Don't get depressed. These are just thoughts to awaken us so we ask ourselves, "What am I doing?"

I am leading you to yama and niyama. You need to understand this before you can get to yama and niyama.

So the sage says, "Right now, the most responsible thing you can do is to withdraw from unconscious activity, but withdrawing from activity is not so simple."

For example, we've tried to have breakfast in silence in the ashram. I don't know how successful we've been.

People think, "I've been up since four or five o'clock. I've already taken a walk on the rail trail. I've already done my āsanas. I have been to the temple. The *āratī* is over. The text has been chanted. I've done my ten minutes of token meditation. Now I'm dying to say something! Because I've already been at it for three or four hours."

A few people may go to the Śiva *liṅgam* by the stream and sit there. They listen to the water flowing. If someone approaches, they think, "Go away. I like the noise I have in my own head. I want to listen to that before I listen to you giving me more noise."

You may see these people and think, "What are they doing?"

This is why the sage says withdrawing is not so simple. He says, "It takes tremendous maturity to simply sit quietly."

Some people tell me, "Who will do it if I don't do it?"

My question is, if you die now, will your family say, "Oh my God, who will take care of us now?"

No. They will burn you or bury you. They will dispose of you. And then they will go on with life. They will put a picture up and say, "He was a very nice person." That's it. Their life won't stop. Nobody's life stops. Nobody pauses for long.

The Indian tradition says one should mourn for thirteen days. But today everybody says, "I don't have time for thirteen days. How can I mourn for thirteen days? And what do I mourn about? My loved one is gone. So for whom should I mourn?"

The mourning is actually for you. It is for you, so you realize the same thing is going to happen to you one day.

The sage says that withdrawing from activity does not come as the result of being lazy or irresponsible. He says, "It comes because you are aware and conscious."

If we think now about the yamas and niyamas, we understand that they must be done with awareness, with consciousness.

Discipline is important in each and every one's life.

Humans may think, "I don't need discipline." But all of us who've had dogs know how you train a dog. For example, you train him to know that you will take him for a walk at 5:00 a.m. Over time, the dog will come and sit at the foot of your bed at 4:58 or 4:59 and go, "Arrr-rrrr." He is telling you that you need to go to the bathroom and brush your teeth. He's saying, "We need to get going!" He gives you a five-minute warning, like an alarm clock.

You say, "Shh, shut up! I want to sleep."

For a moment he says, "Okay. Fine." But then he licks your feet or your face. The next thing you know, he is on top of you, looking at you, as if he's saying, "Are we going or not? It's past five fifteen now!"

Or you have a cow, and you milk it at 5:00 a.m. and 5:00 p.m., or 4:00 a.m. and 4 p.m. Suppose you miss the time by ten minutes, fifteen minutes. You walk into the place where the cow is tied up. It's crying, "Moo!" It's telling you, "It's time!"

So a yogi says, "Become disciplined." This is where the yamas and niyamas come in.

THE YAMAS

The yamas refer to the attitude we must have toward external things and people. The niyamas refer to the internal observances we must follow. Of course, the attitude for the yamas also comes from within.

In *sūtra* thirty of the *Yoga Sūtras*, Patañjali lists the yamas: *ahiṁsā, satya, asteya, brahmacharya, aparigraha*. What do the yamas mean? Ahiṁsā is harmlessness. Satya means speaking the truth. Asteya means not stealing. Brahmacharya means moving toward the highest Truth. Aparigraha means not taking, not seizing.

We start with ahiṁsā. This is the quality Mahatma Gandhi was known for around the world. The definition used is nonviolence. Dr. Martin Luther King, Jr. took the teaching of nonviolence and applied it in his movement.

Ahiṁsā is *a* and *hiṁsā*. *Hiṁsā* means cruelty. In Sanskrit, when you see an *ā* or an *a* at the beginning of a word, it means no. Ahiṁsā is not just avoiding physical actions so you don't hurt somebody on the outside, but it is actually changing your entire thought process so it becomes nonviolent. That is the true meaning of harmlessness. Your thought itself is peaceful.

A yogi would say, "Pay attention to what you consume as food." Because food is what creates thought. Food is what creates dreams. Therefore a *sāttvic*, or pure and uplifting, diet is important.

You can't just say, "I'll become nonviolent" or "I'll become harmless." You have to look at your thought process, the food you eat, the company you keep, the movies you see, the music you listen to, and all of that, in order to achieve ahiṁsā.

The second is satya. I'm sure many in this world think, "I speak the truth. I only speak the truth. I never speak anything but the truth."

In the *Śrīmad Bhagavad Gītā*, Lord Kṛṣṇa is clear when he says speech should not just be truthful, it should be pleasing to the ear and it should be beneficial as well.

When you tell something to someone, he should be pleased to hear what you are saying and he should also be uplifted. You can't just speak the truth, thinking, "I don't care what you feel." Then you have not told the truth, because you have done hiṁsā. You've been violent. You've been harmful.

The sage would say, "Just be silent." It is difficult, I know. You have to take a big breath. Over time, you realize your whole thought process and your speech have to become linked. Everything goes back to your thoughts: "O my mind, have noble thoughts. Have auspicious thoughts." If you have noble and auspicious thoughts, then what you speak will also be noble and auspicious.

Yoga teaches the discipline of speech. You come to a place within yourself where you don't speak too much. You only speak a little, but what little you say comes true. This is because your speech is imbued with *śakti*, power. Your speech is connected to the divinity within.

This occurs over a period of time. Don't think that if you're silent for twenty-four hours, your speech will be powerful tomorrow.

But try, sometimes, to be silent. And try not only to be silent through the mouth but to be silent in the mind also. Try to have fewer thoughts.

Now, asteya. *Steya* means stealing. So asteya is not stealing. We should not take things that don't belong to us, things to which we are not entitled.

Normally we go to a shop, we pick up something, and we pay for it. But if we pick up something, put it in our bag, and walk out, that's called shoplifting. You can see it on the security camera.

The next is brahmacharya. Many people think of brahmacharya simply as celibacy, as not having sexual relations. But the sages describe it as "grazing in the Absolute," as walking toward Brahman."

Therefore, we form relationships that foster the understanding of the great Truth. We keep the company of those who talk about the Truth.

I often use the example of Swami Brahmānanda Mahārāj.

We sat in his company when he was eighty. We were in our thirties, so he was almost fifty years our senior. He would sit with his books, and people would come. He would put his book down, take his glasses off, and say, "How are you? What is going on?"

Sometimes the person would begin to gossip.

Over time, I realized Mahārājji never told people not to say what they were saying. Instead, in his gentle way, he led them to a higher conversation. They probably never realized how he had shifted away from gossip or just loose talk to an uplifting conversation of satsaṅg.

I'm sure he didn't even say to himself, "Now I'm going to do this." But because he kept noble company and auspicious thoughts through his study, gossip and loose talk did not hold value. He was able to lead people into a conversation that was uplifting, without ever demeaning them.

When people walked away, they felt uplifted, happy. They felt their problems were solved just by telling Mahārājji. All Mahārājji had done was remind them, "You are the Absolute. You are Truth. You are divine."

So each of us must remember to let our mind always graze in thoughts of the highest Truth. The first three yamas—ahiṁsā, satya, and asteya—happen automatically when the mind is established in the highest Truth.

The last is aparigraha. It means not taking, not seizing, or taking only that which is necessary.

I'll share two stories.

One happened here in the United States. An armored truck driving on the freeway accidently dropped a brown paper bag—I'll assume it was brown—with cash. How it fell out of an armored truck, I don't know. But this is how I read it.

A person who has no money finds this bag. It has about a hundred thousand US dollars in it. He turns it in.

A news station picks up the story and reports it. The man is asked, "Nobody would have known you found this bag, so why did you turn it in?"

He says, "I have children at home. They would have seen that all of a sudden I have cash. They would ask, 'Where did this come from, Daddy?' At some point, I would have to tell them the truth. I would have to say it's not really mine, I just found it. I realized it is better in the long run that they think I am an honest man. So I did not keep what was not mine."

This is aparigraha, not taking advantage of a situation. Of course, it's tempting. I'm sure the man thought about that. But because his mind had constantly kept good company, he was able to make the decision to return it, knowing that was the best thing to do.

The second story is about Bhagavān Nityānanda.

Behind where his samādhi shrine stands now is a temple to Kṛṣṇa. One day he tells a person, "Go to the temple and empty the donation box. Take sixty percent of the money and leave forty percent."

The person goes there and takes sixty percent and leaves forty percent.

The next morning, he comes to Bhagavān and reports, "The box has been broken into."

Bhagavān says, "That's why I left the forty percent. I knew there would be a break-in, and I knew the person needed money. But he only needed the amount that was left."

This goes back to the matter of satya. You come to a place of truth within yourself. Then what you say comes true. You are able to connect.

Often people say, "I'm going to connect to the Truth." They are like a doctor with a stethoscope. "How am I feeling now? Truth? Let me see. Wait one second, I'm just connecting to the Truth. I can't feel the Truth right now. I'll call you back in an hour. Truth? Not connected yet. Maybe in two hours. No, not connected yet."

They're never connected!

Either you are connected or you're not. Of course, you can fake it till you make it. But don't play games! Don't have your phone in airplane mode and say it's not connecting to the tower.

That's a game people play with themselves.

Similarly, you can't say, "I will follow the yamas on Monday and Thursday and Sunday. And on Tuesday, Wednesday, Friday, and Saturday I'll just be me."

Sometimes people say, "I'm spiritual today. Today I'm holy." Another day they say, "Don't count on me to behave the right way."

The scriptures tell us, "It is only when one puts forth effort that one is able to accomplish something in life." You can't just sit there and use your imagination.

The example given is of a lion. A lion cannot lie there and imagine that food from the forest will come to him. He can't simply dream that a deer will walk into his mouth.

We as humans tend to be like that. We dream, but we don't necessarily make the effort.

The yamas and niyamas require effort. Effort must be put forth every single moment, every single day. To be nonviolent, to be truthful, to graze in Brahman, to not steal, to not want somebody else's things—these are practices the mind must do regularly.

IMMERSED IN THE MANTRA

Namaste. With great respect and love, I'd like to welcome everyone to satsaṅg here this Sunday. Our topic this year has been love, or devotion, and someone recently asked me to speak about mantra and the power of *Oṁ Namaḥ Śivāya.*

Oṁ is considered the primordial sound. It is said that when you take a conch and put it to your ear, in the beginning you hear the ocean. And then as you evolve in your listening, you hear *Oṁ*.

If you've never done this, I advise you to try. Of course, it may take a while to hear the *Oṁ*. You may be waiting for the conch to change. But the conch is not going to change. It is your perception, your listening, that goes through a change.

Mantra is a wonderful subject, and I don't know if we can do justice to it in these few moments. Baba Muktanānda taught that *japa*, or mantra repetition, is an important practice. I would say it's an important practice in every tradition. Japa is done within the Indian tradition, the Muslim tradition, the Christian tradition.

Often people think of it as prayer. Prayer can be considered a gross form of japa. As you continue to do it, the practice becomes more subtle.

Many of you are aware of the four kinds of speech: on the tongue, in the throat, in the heart, and in the navel area. The grossest form of japa is repetition with the tongue. Over time, as you allow yourself to become subtler and more sensitive to your own being, mantra repetition bears fruit.

The very simple meaning of *namaḥ* is salutations. And *śivāya*, which refers to Śiva, is understood as auspiciousness. So we can say *Oṁ Namaḥ Śivāya* means "Salutations to that which is auspicious."

The mind is taught to think noble thoughts, to have auspicious thoughts. In modern terms, we think of this as having positive thoughts. Otherwise, the tendency of the normal mind that hasn't turned to anything uplifting or spiritual is to have negative thoughts, to have thoughts that do not benefit the person who's having those thoughts, or anyone else.

Of all the CDs and tape recordings we have of Baba singing the mantra *Oṁ Namaḥ Śivāya*, I love a particular one from Mahāśivarātri in 1977. I don't know if I was there at that time, but I listen to it a lot. It has a magic that transports you instantly to a place, a world, the mind can only imagine.

When the mind is agitated, it's like being in the spin cycle of a washing machine. I know none of us can sit in a machine that's spinning, but we can imagine looking at one piece of cloth inside the machine on the spin cycle. The mind with the mantra is like that piece of cloth in the spin cycle. If you can live through that spin cycle and come out the other side, then you'll find yourself steady, comfortable, and peaceful within yourself.

I think of chanting, especially chanting the mantra, as a way of cleansing, of purifying, oneself. On the outside, you use shampoo, soap, perfume. But how do you cleanse and purify and make yourself fragrant within? The only way is to allow the mind to become immersed in the mantra.

Baba would talk about becoming pure, cleansing oneself. He would say that through spiritual practice, through keeping good company, through eating pure food, we bring about purification.

It may take 125,000 repetitions or a million repetitions, but finally japa reaches the navel region. Then one is not repeating it oneself. One simply hears it happening.

Many people tell me, "Oh, I don't do the mantra anymore. It happens." Just by looking at these people, you know whether japa is happening on its own or the mantra is just being repeated.

Baba used to tell a story about a disciple who goes to the Guru. He says, "I want wisdom."

The Guru says, "*Tat tvam asi*. You are That."

He says, "That's all?"

The Guru says, "That's it."

The disciple says, "Ah, it's too simple." So he goes to the ashram down the road.

The Guru there is a little bit street smart, we would say. He asks the disciple, "Where have you been? Whom have you met?"

He says, "I was just with that other Guru. What he said was too simple."

This Guru says, "Okay. Here you will have to work for me for twelve years."

Then the Guru calls his manager. The manager and the Guru know how to handle this situation, so the Guru says to the manager, "This boy wants wisdom, but I've told him he first has to work here for twelve years. What work can he do?"

In Baba Muktānanda's time, the best *sevā*, or service, was to work in the cowshed picking up cow dung. So this manager says, "All the sevās are full right now. The only one that is available is picking up cow dung in the cowshed."

The Guru asks the man, "Well, are you willing to do that?"

He says, "For knowledge, I'm willing to do anything."

So for twelve years he's in the cowshed picking up cow dung. He counts the days, counts the hours, counts the time. When his twelve years are up, he comes to the Guru and says, "Now give me knowledge. I have worked here for twelve years."

The Guru says, "*Tat tvam asi*. You are That."

He says, "Wait a minute. I got this for free from that other Guru, and you made me work here for twelve years picking up cow dung?"

And the Guru says, "The Truth has not changed in twelve years. The Truth was, the Truth is, and the Truth will always be the same."

When we actually think about it, we realize it is simple.

We have the Śiva liṅgam by the stream down there. When you go and sit there on a warm day, it is a simple experience. You are there. There is the stream. There are the trees. There is nothing special to see. It is what it is.

The mantra is also simple. "I offer salutations to auspiciousness." You think, "That's all? There must be a greater meaning."

But what greater meaning can there be other than to always have auspicious thoughts, uplifting thoughts, noble thoughts, and for the mind to always be humble and always offer salutations?

When you really think about it, how often are you really humble? How often are you really and truly offering salutations? It takes so much effort to bring the two palms together and say, "Namaste."

A month ago, the Wallkill River was dry. You could see the rocks because it hadn't rained. Then it rained and it filled up. In the same way, we must rain within constantly for our reservoir to be full, so that somebody can take from there and so that we have something to give.

The syllables of the mantra you repeat redeem you. They free you, first of all, from your own thought process. When the Guru gives you a mantra, it is to replace all the other thoughts you have with one thought.

When things happen in life, we have our own choice of words to express frustration, and they are not usually uplifting words. Along with them, most people usually say, "Sorry." The frustration has been expressed through a word they know is not correct, and they realize, "Now I'm not looking so glamorous in front of this person, because I've used a word that's not appropriate." If they had used an auspicious word, they wouldn't have to say, "Sorry." So the practice the Guru encourages is to use auspicious words even in frustrating moments.

The easiest way to explain this is with a story about King Akbar and Birbal. A man comes to court and says, "I can speak twenty languages, so you'll never find out where I'm from."

King Akbar is a little perplexed. This is a challenge. He's the emperor of Delhi, so how can he not know where this person is from?

Birbal tells the guest, "You are such a great man. You must accept our hospitality and spend the night with us."

When the man is fast asleep that night, Birbal comes in with a pitcher of cold water and pours it on his face.

When the man feels the water, he cries out in his native

language. Of course, this is all done secretly, so the man does not realize it is Birbal.

The next morning, when the court gathers, Birbal tells him, "You are from this state, from this place, and you speak this language."

The man is aghast. How could they figure it out?

The sages tell us that our true nature goes with us everywhere we go. Therefore, Baba would say, "Wherever you go, you go."

You can come here or go somewhere, and act very holy. But the situations that arise in life reveal how much mantra repetition you have done, how much meditation you have done, and how much understanding has become a part of you.

Jñāneśvar Mahārāj says, "Constantly repeat the name of the Lord. We cannot count the amount of merit that is gained by simply chanting the name of God."

Baba would tell people when they cooked in his ashram, "Chant, sing." Many modern kitchens have a television, so the cook is watching it while microwaving the food. But Baba would say, "Put that vibration into the food. Don't play other music, don't do other things."

The mantra begins as a thought within you. And that thought filters throughout your being. If you've ever had an Āyurvedic oil massage, you have seen that they use a lot of oil. You may wonder why so much oil. They say that it takes that much to actually get into all the layers of the skin. Similarly, the subtlety of the mantra has to spread throughout the body—through every pore, to every single cell.

I always remember that Baba talked about meeting a *sādhu* in Karnataka during his traveling days. He said to the sādhu, "Please speak to me about the power of the mantra."

The sādhu had his shoes lying there. He said to Baba, "Pick up that shoe. Put it by your ear."

When Baba did that, the sādhu said, "What do you hear?"

Baba said, "*Oṁ Namaḥ Śivāya*."

The sādhu said, "Now you can put the shoe down. You have

experienced the power of the mantra."

The various things you own are inert, but they should become filled with that sound. When somebody picks up your object, it should not stink, it should have the fragrance of the mantra.

Where Baba is buried used to be his meditation room and also at one time his bedroom. After he moved to his bigger apartment, that room stayed locked for twelve years. Every so often, when he felt somebody needed a big jolt, he would tell us, "Take this person to that room."

The person would have no instructions and no information, no knowledge, about where he was being sent. There was a cushion, and we would leave the person there.

Sometimes an hour or two or three later, Baba would say, "Oh, go get him."

Then we would go, and it would take a few moments to bring that individual back and say, "Baba wants to see you." Because the person would still be in another world. He would say, "I sat there, and the walls began repeating the mantra."

People chant for a short time and say, "Okay, I'm done." But a sage sits for what seems to us like a long time and immerses himself in the practice of mantra. The room could have a brick wall or a sheetrock wall, it doesn't matter. Those walls become filled with japa.

Baba often said that when you lie down for fifteen minutes after your morning meditation, the rest you get for those fifteen minutes is better than six hours of sleep. I can vouch for that. Especially in his later years, Baba made it a practice. When he was done with his other practices in the morning, he would send everybody away and have fifteen minutes of just rest. It is a way of spreading that energy through the body, of gathering oneself and saying, "Okay, now I'm ready for the day."

Jñāneśvar says, "Who can describe the incomparable fortune of the person whose tongue is dedicated to the name of the Lord, which is the essence of all scriptures?"

Imagine that when you wake up in the morning from a good

sleep, your mind is not thinking "orange juice" or "coffee." It is not thinking cigarette, cigar, or whatever. Instead, the mind is thinking, "I want to sing. I want to chant."

An easy way today is to set the alarm on your smart phone or iPod or other device so it doesn't go beep, beep, beep, beep, beep but plays a chant you love. Whether you want it or not, the first sound the ears hear is a chant. So automatically, the mind thinks of the power of mantra.

Our father woke us up in childhood by playing Baba's *Guru Gītā*. Most days we had to get up and get ready for school. But once in a while, I'd be home on a weekend, and I'd think, "Okay, today I can sleep in." But then I would hear the *Gītā* playing. The tape recorder was right outside my room, so I would get up to turn it off. And it would already be off. It had not been set. I learned over time to laugh at this.

The practice of mantra repetition, as Baba would say, becomes so much a part of you that nobody has to remind you to do it. It just is what happens. That is the place we want to arrive at—where, as he says, "the tongue is dedicated to the name of the Lord."

Jñāneśvar says, "They are rare who chant the name, the mantra, incessantly."

So if you think, "I chant a lot," think again. He means chant nonstop. In our world today, that would be twenty-four hours a day, seven days a week.

The best thing to do over these winter months is to find some periods of time when there is no television, no Internet, no distractions. Sit in your favorite chair or in your favorite spot, or in front of a fire, and allow yourself to chant the mantra.

Don't get up. Because as soon as you get up, the flow is lost. So whatever your bodily needs are, take care of those first. Take a minimum of thirty minutes if you tend to be restless. Or if you think of yourself as a mature, serious, spiritual seeker, then two hours will seem like nothing. Make it a practice not to look at the clock because then you think, "Okay, now it's one hour and fifty-nine minutes," and the last minute will feel like an hour.

You might say, "I don't have time. I can't do that. It's not possible."

It may never seem possible, but you have to make it possible. You have to think to yourself, "What is it that I'm willing to give up? What is it that I'm willing to let go? What is there that I'm ready to say, 'It's okay if I don't do it'?" That is the choice you have to make.

I hope and pray that you'll try this over the next few months, while the weather is cold outside and you're not rushing to get out in the snow, except to go to work and come back home. It gets dark early. So instead of getting depressed and all the other things that come with early sunset, think, "I have a project. I want to become still. I want to become steady. I don't want to crave. I don't want to grieve. I don't want to hate. I don't want to run after a pleasure. Rather, I want to become still within myself."

Offer salutations. Have auspicious thoughts. It's a tall order. That's a lot to do over six months. But it goes by fast. Before you know it, spring will be here.

Mīrābāī was a queen from the northwestern state of Rajasthan in India and she awakened to the love of Kṛṣṇa. She would go to the temple and she would hang out with the local people and just be immersed in her singing, in her devotion, in her love.

She talks to her own mind and tells it, "Drink the nectar of the name of God. Give up bad company. Sit in good company. Listen to the glories of God. Let the mind become free of desire, of anger, of arrogance, of greed, of attachment. Let all of these things just go away. Mīrā says, 'Let the mind become filled with the essence of the Lord.'"

So let us all, over these next few months, allow our mind and our senses and our whole being to become filled with that love.

I AM NOT THE BODY

With great respect and love, I would like to welcome everyone to satsaṅg here this morning. As we were chanting, I felt like it was only last week that we were here together. It didn't seem like three or four months since we've all gotten together.

Since the beginning of the year, we have been studying the *Aṣṭāvakra Gītā*.

In his commentary, Swami Chinmayānandaji warns seekers that such scriptures can only truly be understood when a person has contemplated, meditated on, and become rooted in the vivid experience of transcendental oneness. If the mind has not been purified and we engage in such study or meditation, a book with this kind of wisdom doesn't really help us.

In fact, he says, if a student is not situated in this wisdom, this knowledge, it can blast his faith. It can shake his grasp of the highest reality.

Most of the scriptures we study are in the form of conversations, or dialogues, between the teacher and the student. Formal classes are probably no longer than an hour, so the remaining twenty-three hours of the day are for study, contemplation, conversations with oneself, conversations with fellow seekers… and then, again, quiet contemplation by oneself.

The philosophy of the *Aṣṭāvakra Gītā* tells us, "I am not the body; I am Consciousness."

It is not easy to eliminate the thought "I am the body." All our dealings in society, in life, are through the body. So whenever we relate to something, we don't naturally say, "I am Consciousness." We say, "*I* am going to do that." Or "*I* will be there."

I have often shared how Bhagavān Nityānanda spoke about himself. Instead of saying "I'm going to…," he would say, "This body is going to…." It sounds strange to us because, though it is a concept we find in the *Aṣṭāvakra Gītā* or the Avadhūta Stotram or other scriptures, it's not how we feel. It's not a direct experience within.

We chant in Ādi Śaṅkarācārya's "Six Stanzas of Salvation," "I am not the mind. I am not the breath. I am not all of these things. I am simply Consciousness. I am Śiva. I am that universal Self." As a concept, this sounds good. But when you're in society and you're speaking with people, it's not always an easy concept to sit in.

Based on the teaching Aṣṭāvakra gives to King Janaka, we can't say, "So-and-so turned fifty this week." We would have to say, "That body turned fifty this week." Of course, whenever I say something like that, people like to have a little fun with the words.

It's winter right now, so when you meet people, they discuss the cold. When I was getting ready to leave Magod, some people said, "But you're going to the snow!" In Magod, it's sixty degrees; it's comfortable. The mind always thinks about obstacles and problems rather than about how we can enjoy what is.

I'm sure that when we return again in July, somebody will say, "Oh, it's so hot! Can't wait for the fall!" And now, while it's winter, people can't wait to go to the Bahamas or Florida or Hawaii, or wherever.

When you study the scriptures, you realize it all ultimately boils down to the mind. It has nothing to do with the weather. It has nothing to do with anybody or any thing. It has to do with who I think I am.

Even though, as I said, it feels like it was only last Sunday that we gathered here, of course, at some level I know we were in Magod last week and had satsaṅg there. The satsaṅg was in English because the Level II hatha yoga course was going on. Some people had questions. One was "How come we can't love those whom we are closest to; why aren't we nice to them?" The second was "Can I have a blessing during darśan?" The third was a question many people probably ponder: "When I'm away from the ashram or from others who go to satsaṅg, when I am alone by myself, how do I remain established in the teachings? How do I stay connected?"

Sage Aṣṭāvakra tells King Janaka in answer to his questions, "All of the answers come to me as I practice." Swami

Chinmayānanda tells us to become established in our daily practice of meditation.

KNOWLEDGE COMES FROM WITHIN

King Janaka begins with what we might call some simple questions to Aṣṭāvakra. He says, "How do I acquire this knowledge? How can liberation come about? How is renunciation achieved?"

Sometimes people wonder, "What does renunciation mean? Does it mean I have to leave my family? Does it mean I have to leave my friends?"

These questions arise when we think about renunciation, but the sages tell us renunciation is about learning to detach from our own perceptions, feelings, and thoughts. We realize, "I am simply caught in the way I perceive. I am simply caught in the way I listen. I am simply caught in what I see and what I hear and what I feel."

Somebody smiles at us, and we like it. Somebody else doesn't smile, and we begin to worry. The night I left, a man came to visit me in Mumbai. He came in and greeted me and greeted all those who were nearby.

A woman was sitting in one corner of the room, and when he walked out again, she said to me, "He never saw me."

I said, "Correct. He never saw you in that corner. He came for a purpose; that purpose was done, and he walked out."

She was able to smile and laugh. But what she does when she sees him next I can't guarantee. "You never saw me that day. You only saw him and those around him. What about me in the corner?"

According to the sage, renunciation in this moment is coming to the realization that what happened has nothing to do with anything except your own concepts. It is nothing personal. He simply didn't look in the corner before he went out. But the mind will not forget that evening, that moment. The mind holds onto it.

How do we contemplate this question asked by Janaka: "How can knowledge be acquired?" In the example I just described, knowledge is acquired the instant you realize it was nothing personal. This is the vital knowledge in that moment—not "I am the Self, I am bliss, I am Consciousness." Of course, the knowledge "I am the Self, I am bliss, I am Consciousness" must always remain, but in that moment, the knowledge you need is "It's nothing personal."

When somebody asks, "How are you?" we do a quick scan to see if we are going to say, "I'm happy" or the opposite. Usually most of us say, "Well, today is good" because we don't want to discuss too much about what's really going on. We want to just get it over with. Now, if it's a really good friend, we say, "Let's have a cup of chai or tea or coffee and discuss what's really going on."

The sage tells us to come to the realization that none of that truly matters. All of it is simply a game of the mind and intellect, a game of the emotions.

If we sit and we contemplate, at some point we are able to become a witness. We observe that we are caught in all of this because of our own mind. If we happen to have that realization, we are able to laugh.

Of course, it's not easy. On the one hand, yes, we have the realization "I am the Self, I am Consciousness." On the other hand, we think, "All that is fine, *but…*"

Today it's a nice, fifty-degree day. A little windy. Tomorrow it might be something else. You tell yourself, "Maybe I can call God and say, 'I'm going to New York City tomorrow. I'd like no snow, please. I'd like the sun to shine. I'd like the weather to remain amicable to my driving because I don't like driving on black ice.'"

God calls you back and says, "Okay, I have checked the records, and for you I can arrange that."

We are funny in that way, you know?

If you really think about it, it is what it is. The only thing you can do is accept it and become comfortable within yourself. You, the individual, must come to accept "This is who and what I am." This is knowledge.

Knowledge doesn't come from anywhere else, anything else, anyone else. It comes from within.

Who you are, what you are, and the baggage you have

brought along with you shift slowly over time. Everything changes. But you remain you. That is a great illumination, if you can accept it.

Some people come to the ashram and say, "I'm spending three months here this summer, and by the end I'll have gotten everything." Or they say, "I'm going to gather all the knowledge at the retreat, and I'll go home with everything."

Congratulations! But fifty years from now, will you still have it? I think it would be great if you could just get to know "I am not the body."

They say, "I'm on the fast track to liberation."

Maybe that's why King Janaka's first question is "How do I acquire this knowledge?" And he's probably also thinking, "Okay, got it! Easy! I'm going to get there."

But then we wonder how much did Janaka really get? Of course, the sages tell us that while living in the kingdom and doing his job as king, he remains detached from his body, from his mind.

Aṣṭāvakra teaches him, "O king, just as the shape of a temple does not affect the sky, the crookedness of the physical body has no effect on the Ātman, or the soul that dwells within." Aṣṭāvakra's body was crooked in eight places.

Aṣṭāvakra says, "A wise person looks at the reality behind this manifested world, whereas an ignorant one gets lost in names and forms."

This is the knowledge that Aṣṭāvakra gives to King Janaka that allows him to understand that he is the Self, and that he is not the physical body or any of that which is constantly changing.

THE BEST IS TO BE QUIET

Only when the ego feels incomplete does the sense of attachment arise. Knowing this, we can see what fights are about in this life. When the ego is not satisfied or is not given attention, one sits in the corner and the ego feels, "Why was I not seen? I'm just as important in this situation."

I have seen over time that some people make sure they cover all their bases. They make the effort to say hello to every single person in a room. Everyone loves these kinds of people. The other type of person realizes that saying hello individually does not really make a difference. That type of person already feels the connection within himself. We could say one type is socially correct, and the other is doing what is correct for that person.

When I left Magod, I said, "Okay, I have to go. So we'll all stand up together and have darśan together." And then, boom, I left.

I'm sure some people thought, "Oh my God, he's leaving for a month. I didn't get a chance to say…."

But I thought, "I was there for three months, and we met each other every single day. Whatever it is could have been said yesterday or the day before."

Still, people want to say, "Have a good trip. We'll see you when you come back." Of course, I know that. I will have a good trip. And I will see them when I come back… if they're still around.

It's funny if you see it that way. I've taught myself that I must see it that way. If one doesn't have that view, the mind tends to get upset very quickly.

To have knowledge, you must realize that the whole world, as Baba Muktānanda said, is nothing but a big stage upon which we are all actors.

What is knowledge? Knowledge is having the realization that the Self, which dwells within, is playing all these roles. Yet we get caught in the role that is being played. We get caught in whatever is happening to us in that role.

What does the sage do? He is able to stand back and witness

the drama.

But we think, "Oh no, wait a minute. Let me make sure everything is as it should be."

No. It is as it is. It is as it will be.

What can you really do? You are nice. You are sweet. You are loving. You are kind. You are doing all the right things. Still, somebody gets upset. So you think, "Let me go and explain why I was nice, why I was kind, why I was compassionate."

However, it is not in that person's nature or personality to respond differently. He is caught in his own perceptions, feelings, and thoughts.

I often think of a sculptor. He sits before a stone, with his chisel and hammer, and he is constantly chiseling away. If a seeker can understand this image, he realizes that over time he has been hardened by his own views, emotions, and thoughts. So the process of contemplation—of *viveka*, or discrimination—is to take your hammer and chisel and to knock away all of that. Then you know "I am not the body."

Every Sunday at Magod we sing the "Six Stanzas of Salvation." As we sing, I sometimes laugh to myself. I laugh with the thought that the sage is reminding us, "I am not… not… not… not… not…."

Some people don't like the philosophy of negation. They say, "It's too negative."

But Ādi Śaṅkarācārya gives a very important teaching in the refrain. He says, "I am Consciousness. I am bliss. I am the Absolute. I am Śiva."

Although a seeker may begin by realizing "I am not all of this," the foundation upon which that seeker must rest is "I am Consciousness. I am bliss. I am the Absolute. I am Śiva." The mind must constantly remember this. This is knowledge.

Renunciation, the first step, is not getting caught. And liberation is becoming established in the experience of "I am Consciousness. I am bliss. I am the Absolute. I am Śiva." That's how simple the answer to this question is.

Of course, as long as we live in this world of duality, we can't avoid the sense of attachment. We have likes and dislikes. We love, and we don't love. In this way, the mind creates duality. It creates questions about what we want and don't want, and then it gets caught in those questions.

Somebody gives a smart answer, and we think, "Wow, he's wise." Somebody else doesn't give an answer, and we wonder, "Did he even understand my question?"

I often think that when somebody doesn't answer, he's actually being wise. He simply smiles because he realizes that if he answers one way, he will get caught, and if he answers another way, he will still get caught. He is caught either way.

Therefore, the sage tells us, the best is to be quiet.

If you go to a store, there are thousands of things for sale. You don't buy every single one. You don't buy the entire store. You don't go to the mall and say, "I want everything." Of course, the mind may think, "I want everything."

I always think of the answer the Dalai Lama gave when he was taken to a mall. It was probably on his first visit to the United States. The person was proud to show him, and asked, "What do you think?"

The Dalai Lama said, "All things I don't need."

The person of wisdom, faced with the question "What can I take and what can I not take?" comes to the realization that none of this is actually needed.

Recently somebody sent me a joke. A traveler visits a yogi. The yogi is seated in his little hut. He has hardly any belongings. The traveler asks the yogi, "Do you live here?"

The yogi says, "Yes, I live here."

The traveler asks, "Then where are your belongings?"

The yogi asks him, "O traveler, where are your belongings?"

The traveler says, "I don't have any belongings because I am moving from place to place."

The yogi says, "I am also a traveler."

When King Janaka asks, "How is renunciation achieved?" Aṣṭāvakra replies that the objects of the senses must be rejected as poison. He says, "Seek forgiveness, straightforwardness, kindness, cheerfulness, and truth as nectar."

If we remember simply not to get caught in our own mind, intellect, emotions, and feelings, maybe we have attained a little bit of what the sage wishes to express to Janaka.

In the *Avadhūta Stotram* we sing, "I am not the body; the body is not me."

A body—as I began by saying—may turn fifty, but the Self that dwells within it is eternal. As long as the Self is in the body, the body seems real. The day the Self leaves that body, then no matter how much it is loved, the body is not kept by anyone.

Some people say, "That's too much to think about."

You cannot do anything to change this. However, as a seeker, you can come to the understanding that all this shall perish one day. You can contemplate: if all this shall perish, then what is it that is real? That is what King Janaka wishes to know. That is what everyone in this room and in every satsaṅg wishes to know.

At some point, or in various moments, we have illuminations. We understand. But then once again, we are caught in the process of our own thoughts, emotions, limitations.

Satsaṅg is not something that happens only on the outside. It must happen within yourself as well. So allow your mind to constantly ruminate upon these teachings. Then, wherever you go, you bring that contemplation with you.

Ultimately, you realize that the most important ingredient in all of this, as Baba Muktānanda always reminded us, is love. Your love has brought you here today, on this beautiful Sunday morning. And now we have the thought of being together over the next few weeks, enjoying satsaṅg. And then again, life goes on.

EQUAL VISION

With great love and respect, I'd like to welcome everyone to our Intensive here this wintery morning.

Our subject is very difficult: equal vision.

The scriptures call it *samadṛṣṭi*, equal vision. Each one of us is very aware that, conceptually, equal vision is a good idea. At least it seems like a good idea. But to actually live it and follow it isn't so easy.

What does it mean to have equal vision? We might be able to speak eloquently about equal vision, about the Truth, but the question boils down to "Can I live it?"

Many people say, "My children won't come to satsaṅg."

I tell them, "It's because you don't follow the teachings. You don't live the teachings. You don't practice the teachings. You preach the teachings, yes. But how much of it do you actually live in your life so that your child is able to see that and say, 'Yes, I want that, and therefore I will come'?"

At that point, parents usually say, "You're right."

Somewhere within yourself, you know this is right. Because the Truth dwells within each one of us, it resonates within. The sages make it clear that the Truth was, is, and will be true. If it only was true before or only is true now or only will be true in the future, it is not the Truth. Then it's transitory. Just like us.

How true is this body, how real is this body? Only for as long as it is alive. Before it's born, it never existed. The moment you die, you are past. That's a sad thought, I know. It's not how you want to begin your Saturday morning. You want to feel "I am always here—I was, am, and will be here."

Yes, in the sense of Consciousness, in the sense of Truth, you were, are, and will be. But in the sense of body, of how you know yourself now—no.

Just in this last month, many disciples of Baba Muktānanda have passed away. All were eighty-plus, so it's natural. When you tell elder devotees that so-and-so passed away, all of a sudden they feel sad—not just because someone passed away but because the reality hits home: "I might be next." Of course, nobody will say that to you. They say, "I'm ready. I want to go." But at the same time, they've bought insurance, they've found the best doctors, they've done everything to make sure they'll live as long as possible. Actually, the most important thing is to stay healthy. They don't always think about that.

This topic of equal vision is easy to understand conceptually and intellectually. But it's not so easy to do when you go out into life, into your day-to-day activities, and have to deal with all kinds of nonsensical people. I had to add "nonsensical" because dealing with nonsensical people can immediately take away equal vision.

The question arises: "Why don't those people get it?" Some say it's because of the capability of their brain. You can't talk to a kindergarten child about the subject matter of a PhD. Yet I think when we talk about realizing the Truth, age doesn't matter. In many traditions, we see children who realize the Truth right when they are born. We hear about people of different ages, different lifestyles, different circumstances who get it.

The questions I ask myself instead are "Why do they get it? How do they get it? When do they get it? What makes it possible for people to get it?"

We all have moments when we get it. The philosophy of the *Vijñāna Bhairava* says that every morning when you wake up, for a fleeting, brief, passing moment, you have an experience of the Self. You're just coming out of sleep; your mind is not quite awake. You haven't fully woken up to "I am" whatever it is you identify as. It's probably a state everybody wants to be in, especially on a cold morning like today.

The sages say that in that moment, we are closest to the Self. In that moment, possibly we experience equal vision. But then the mind wakes up. The eyes wake up. The body wakes up. And the concept of equal vision fades.

Don't get sad. Everybody is looking serious here this morning.

The poet-saint Kabīr says, "I am complete." He has the experience of fullness, of wholeness, of completion. There is no sense of lack.

We can talk about when equal vision comes, or when we have arrived at equal vision, but Baba Muktānanda would say that there is no arriving, there is nothing to be discovered, there is nothing to be found. It is already there. It is simply that the sun rises, and in that light, darkness is gone. All of a sudden you realize, “Wow, I always knew it.”

COMPASSION, FORGIVENESS, STRAIGHTFORWARDNESS

I often share a Zen story about two monks—one younger, one older—who live in a forest monastery. The younger monk only has one eye.

To stay in that monastery, one must win a debate. That is the fee.

One day, a visitor comes, and the older monk tells the younger monk, "Debate with this guest. But do it in silence."

The older monk thinks a debate in silence is safe because the younger monk is not so wise. He is new, and when you are new, you think you know a lot, you're hot. The older monk also tells the guest, "Please debate with the younger monk in silence."

So the two meet. They bow to each other.

The guest raises one finger.

The younger monk is a little upset, but he thinks, "I'll be nice to this guest." He raises two fingers.

The guest raises three fingers.

The younger monk raises his fist.

The guest places an apple in front of the younger one, bows, and goes away.

As the guest is hurrying out, the older monk, who is sitting on the porch, says, "Wait! Tell me what happened!"

The guest says, "I lost the debate. I raised one finger, saying, 'There is one God.' The younger monk raised two fingers, saying, 'There is God and there is His creation.' So I raised three fingers: 'Yes, there is God, there is His creation, and there are all of us.' So the younger monk raised his fist, saying, 'It all comes from one Consciousness: God, creation, us, everything.' So, accepting defeat, I placed a piece of fruit in front of him, I bowed, and now I shall move on."

Then the younger monk comes out. He's hot, very angry, upset, looking all around. "Where is he? Where is he?"

The older monk says, "Wait! Tell me what happened!"

He says, "You can't believe how he insulted me!"

The older monk says, "But what happened?"

He says, "First of all, he had the audacity to raise one finger and tell me I had only one eye. I thought I'd be kind and tell him that God is kind and has given him two eyes. And can you believe it: he raised three fingers, saying that between the two of us, there are only three eyes! So I raised my fist. I wanted to punch him! He got so scared that he left a piece of fruit, bowed, and ran away. Now I have to get a hold of him!"

The older monk, like us, laughs.

The scriptures say, "As is your understanding, so is your vision."

I think of Bhagavān Nityānanda, who would sit in silence, total stillness. He would sit and simply observe all that was happening.

Of course, we always want to fix something, to pitch in. But I think, no matter who you are, where you are, where you live, what you do—this knowledge, this equal vision, is there. The only thing each of us has to do is tap into it.

Many years ago, I memorized the first part of a verse in the ninth chapter of the *Bhagavad Gītā* because I thought it was so excellent. *Samo 'haṁ sarvabhūteṣu na me dveṣyo 'sti na priyaḥ*. Kṛṣṇa says, "Consciousness is the same in all. None is dear or hateful to me."

When we talk about equal vision, we must understand this.

In my fifty-three years of existence and thirty-five years of doing this work, I have seen that although Consciousness exists in everything everywhere, more than ninety-five percent of the human population chooses to deny the existence of Consciousness and simply dwells within the human body. For argument's sake, let's say five percent are different; actually, I think it's more like one percent.

These days, we can know in seconds what happens in any part of the world. Even if we didn't know a person existed in some other country, all of a sudden something happens there and we know within a moment. We hear about all the atrocities that are taking place.

The question to ask is "If there is equal vision, if there is understanding about the oneness of Consciousness, then why do human beings still behave in this manner?"

I think the only conclusion is that ninety-five percent or more choose to live in darkness, choose to be dead to this understanding. They choose not to practice compassion. They choose not to practice forgiveness. They choose not to be straightforward. Even those who profess to be compassionate, to be forgiving, to be straightforward—how much do they really feel that within themselves?

People say, "You're so sweet. You're so nice. You're so kind!"

You have to ask yourself, "Am I *really* sweet? Am I really kind? Am I really? Or when I open the door to someone, do I just think, 'Let me make myself presentable.'"

It's easy to think that if you make your hair or face presentable, then all your other qualities will also become presentable. But as soon as something happens, all those qualities vanish. Sorry, but this is the truth. A few heads are nodding, so that means you know this is true.

How do you know if you are really living with equal vision? If you have compassion, forgiveness, straightforwardness.

Suppose you're fast asleep, tired after a long day. Somebody calls you or knocks on your door. You wake up. If your response in that moment is "What can I do? How can I help? Is there anything I can do?" then you know you are moving toward equal vision, straightforwardness, compassion, forgiveness.

But instead you say, "Wait a minute! Didn't you know I was fast asleep?!"

Of course the person knew you were fast asleep. It was obvious because it's the middle of the night. Or it was obvious as soon as you opened the door.

Your response in the moment shows if you are really compassionate, forgiving, loving, kind. Otherwise, you are all of these things from 9 a.m. to 6 p.m., and then 6 p.m. to 9 a.m., you are just yourself.

When you study Vedānta, the first question that arises is "Do you believe in the existence of the all-pervasive

Consciousness?"

The student has to tell the teacher, "Yes, I believe in the existence of the all-pervasive Consciousness."

If the student agrees, then the teacher says, "Okay, now we have the possibility of moving forward."

When you go to college, the first question you are asked is "What are you going to major in?" In our day in India, people asked, "Are you going into the arts? Or the sciences? Or commerce?" Those were the three fields from which you could choose. You couldn't say, "I'll see as I go along." No, the day you applied, you had to decide. Clarity within that field could come as you went along, but you had to make that initial choice.

Equal vision has nothing to do with the eyes seeing. It has to do with an understanding within yourself. *Samo 'haṁ sarvabhūteṣu na me dveṣyo 'sti na priyaḥ*. The mind has to constantly remember "Consciousness exists equally within each and every one." It is not an idea or a concept but an awareness that must be present in your mind at all times. Whether you believe it or not is secondary.

Whenever you get angry or upset, you can tell yourself, "I'm being stupid right now. I'm being an idiot right now. I'm angry right now. I'm upset right now. But deep within myself, I am aware that Consciousness exists equally within all, at all times."

If you are able to hold that thought, I think you have already arrived. Just as the hand is getting ready to punch, the thought arises. And the hand slowly goes down.

In that moment, viveka—the ability to differentiate between what is wise and what is unwise—has arisen. When that happens, you know that your practice is bearing fruit. You may not have equal vision yet, but at least you didn't punch. You don't have to say, "Why did I even raise my fist? Why did I even get upset?" Just be pleased with yourself in that moment. You can smile to yourself and say, "Got it!"

Even though I say ninety-five percent or more of us do

not benefit from or use the teachings, the teachings are not something uncommon. It is natural to know you want to treat someone in the same manner you want to be treated, to be nice to others just as you want others to be nice to you, to be loving to others just as you want others to be loving to you. We know all of this, yet we get caught in a moment of, simply put, ignorance. When you look at yourself in retrospect and think, "Damn it, what happened?" that is a moment of viveka.

Those are the moments that are important. And those moments come often in life. Don't think, "When is that moment?" or "When will I know that moment?" That moment is every moment. And in every moment, you must know. You must know in every cell, every pore, every part of you.

HOW DO I BECOME FREE?

The sage Rāmāṇa Maharṣi says, "The 'I' casts off the illusion of 'I,' and yet it remains as 'I.' Such is the paradox of Self-realization."

Right now, if I ask, "How are you doing?" you would probably say, "I'm doing fine. I have a little cold. I have a little cough. I am whatever."

The sage tells us to say, "The body has a cold. The body has a cough." Because we are actually fine: we are Consciousness. So cast off the idea "I have a cough, I have a cold, or I am whatever it is." Think of yourself as that great Consciousness.

I hope you have equal vision. If not, well, there's not really much you can do about it—except to know it's a wonderful thought; it's a wonderful feeling. I believe that in your lowest moments in life, if you can think that equal vision is even a possibility, that will be very uplifting. But you have to have your own experiences, stories, and feelings attached to that greatness, that vastness.

The *Cāndogya Upaniṣad* says, "The Self is as vast as the sky."

The mind can relate to the vastness of the sky. When you think of what is vast, you think of the sky. What is fathomless? You think of the ocean as fathomless. What is everywhere? You think of water as everywhere. So by inference, you come to the experience of Consciousness. What is vast? The sky is vast. What is vast like the sky? Consciousness is vast like the sky.

As I said, each of us has experienced the greatness of Consciousness, of divinity. In such a moment, forgetting everything else, you feel that vastness, that greatness. It's not induced by anyone or anything; it is your own direct experience. It is not equal vision because a sage said it is or because you read about it somewhere; it is what you experience, even if simply for a moment. The mind remembers those moments.

Become firmly rooted in these feelings, in these experiences. When the wind is blowing, it blows away all the dry leaves, yet the trees stay firm, steady. They may move and bend, but the wind cannot blow them away. In the same way, you must become firmly rooted so that when winds blow in your life, you are not uprooted, you are not disturbed; you are steady.

This is one aspect of equal vision. It's not about being inert, dead, or like a rock. Equal vision is about being very alive, very conscious, very moving; it is about having the ability to bend, yet being firmly rooted.

The *Muṇḍaka Upaniṣad* says, "When the mind rests steady and pure, then whatever you desire, those desires are fulfilled, and whatever you think of, those thoughts materialize. So you who desire good fortune, revere the knower of the Self."

The sage is trying to tell you to let the winds blow away all the unnecessary thoughts, the unnecessary wants, needs, desires. That which is real, let it remain. As you become established in Consciousness, thoughts arising from Consciousness will come to fruition. They will materialize not because it's a miracle or magic but because that is what needs to happen.

Frustration arises because you have a fresh desire every single second. All those desires are never fulfilled, never satisfied. Even if one is satisfied, you aren't satisfied because you want something else.

The *Muṇḍaka Upaniṣad* says, "Having realized the Self, the wise find satisfaction. Their evolution complete, at peace and free from longing, they are at one with everything."

This is the essence of equal vision.

In the ashram in Magod, we have two dogs. One is a Rottweiler, the other is a German shepherd. Once he has been tied, the Rottweiler remains tied. He doesn't do anything about it. The German shepherd, on the other hand, always finds a way to free herself. No matter what type of collar we put on her, she gets free. I'm always amazed because I've tightened the collar, I've gotten a harness that goes through her legs, all of that. I can't for the life of me figure out how she gets out.

So I say that these are the two kinds of disciples, or people, in the world. One says, "Okay, I'm tied." The other says, "How do I become free?"

You have to decide which one you are. The possibility for

freedom exists for both. Are you the one who accepts that there is no point in wasting energy and time to figure out how to get out of the leash? Or are you the one who, no matter how well you have been tied, it's only a matter of time before you're able to get out? The choice is yours.

So hold all of the thoughts we've been talking about. Sit with them. I believe that even if you've moved just a millimeter this morning, that's better than nothing. My belief is that the person who came to satsaṅg and the one who leaves must be different. At least don't go worse off. Tell yourself, "Maybe I don't have equal vision, but I know I can get to it. I know the possibility exists."

You can come into the five percent out of the ninety-five percent.

At least throughout the day today, let these two words—equal vision—remain in your consciousness, awareness, thought process. Somehow you will have an illumination within yourself, for yourself.

LIVE THE TRUTH

With great respect and love, I would like to welcome everyone here to our satsaṅg.

No matter where we go, every Sunday we have satsaṅg. The audience changes, the setting changes, the flowers change—each country has its own kinds of flowers. Now it is wonderful to be here and to share these next few months together.

Swami Vishveshwarānanda just spoke to us about the Truth.

Swamiji looks after about fifteen ashrams in India. He is based out of Mumbai and Haridwar, and many, many people come and visit him on a regular basis. No matter where he goes or whom he meets, his talk is always about the Truth.

The great sages we remember are those who didn't just talk about the Truth but who lived it. They spent a long time internalizing the Truth. Their lives were filled with that experience.

When Swamiji arrived yesterday, I realized it has been thirty-five years since I received the garland from Baba Muktānanda. That was at Guru Pūrṇimā, in July of 1981, in South Fallsburg, New York. So it has been thirty-five years of doing this work. People wonder, "How does a relationship last so long?" It's a good question.

Swamiji and I also go back that many years because in October of 1981, his Guru, Mahāmandaleshwar Swami Brahmānandaji Mahārāj, traveled here in the United States and met Baba. Last night we talked about Baba and about Mahārāji. We talked about the simplicity with which holy men live.

Swamiji shared a very simple teaching his Guru gave just before leaving his body. He said, "Your faith in divinity should never waiver." We should become established in that faith.

When I think of Mahārāji, I think of simplicity. If you met him in the bedroom or in the living room, you met the same man. If you met him having breakfast or having lunch, you met the same man. If you met him on stage at a formal program, you met the same man.

You might say, "Of course you met the same person."

But, no, it's not always like that. People wear a mask. They have a façade. They have a role they play. They say, "Let me get ready..." Mahārāji would say simply, "Let's go." He would never say, "I have to check my face" or "I need to check myself." He was ready. As soon as he got up in the morning, he was ready for the day, until he went to bed at night. Even if he had to go onto a stage, he didn't stop to ask, "How do I look?" What mattered to him was "How am I on the inside?"

Some months ago, I read a quote that said, "Friendship with a noble person is like sugar cane."

I don't know if you eat much sugar cane here in New York. But in tropical countries—and in Hawaii and Florida, probably—there's a lot of sugar cane. It is put into a machine that squeezes it, and sweet juice comes out. And when you eat a piece of sugar cane or suck on it, it's sweet. You can cut it into small pieces and then peel off the husk with your teeth. Chewing it is supposed to be good exercise for the teeth. That's what we're told.

No matter how many small pieces you break the sugar cane into, it is always sweet. So this quote is saying that friendship with noble people is like that: no matter what you do to them or how you act with them, only sweetness comes out.

Often when I meet Swamiji, I ask him, "What will happen as we go ahead, as we go into the future?"

On the one hand, it looks as if the world is very bright and many good things are happening. But it is also worrisome because many ancient traditions, cultures, ways of life, and practices have been given up, sacrificed.

Last night I said, "Swamiji, just as we believe in the greatness of those who lived before us—and in whose company we lived and whose grace has been bestowed upon us—the next generation also must look back and feel 'Yes, I lived with somebody worthwhile.'" I said, "We must do something to make that happen."

Swamiji said, and I also believe, that we pray that some of those qualities of greatness have been imbibed by us. We pray that we carry this sweetness; this love; this ānanda, or joy, with us wherever we go. No matter when or where somebody comes and tells us, "Let's go," we should be able to say, "Yes, we're ready. Let's go."

As we live in these times today, I feel this understanding is even more necessary. I recently heard somebody say that people's negative actions cause less danger than is caused when good people don't perform any actions. Think about this. If you consider yourself a good person or an uplifting person or a peaceful person—whatever label you want to use—not doing something is the most negative, harmful thing you can do.

So let's remind ourselves, "How much can I do?" How great you will become is not important. What is important is how much you can do in this world.

DON'T BECOME THE SOAP

Last summer, we talked about samadṛṣṭi and *samabhāva*, the experience of oneness and of equal vision. And we had a discussion a few days ago in which we asked, "Is this real? Can I be the same at all times?"

This is a question I ask myself. No matter who says what, no matter what happens, no matter the situation, can I always remain established in the Truth and not be affected? Thirty-five years later, I can say, "Yes, I'm better at it."

Still, sometimes I might feel a need to fake it. It's just human nature that you want to react when you feel slightly agitated. But you tell yourself, "No, be established in the Truth." You take a deep breath, or maybe go off to your own room, and say, "Okay, I'm going to find the Truth again."

I think of the cycles in a washing machine. The cloth remains the same whether it is being washed, whether it is being agitated, or whether it is in the spin cycle. Whatever the machine is doing, the cloth remains the same.

I always say, "That's what we need to become."

The world spins you. The world agitates you. The world's turbo power does whatever it does. You just remain the same. This is the fruit and the outcome of satsaṅg.

I think social media is beneficial in the sense that people are using it to share satsaṅg as well. At least the words from satsaṅg are being thrust out to the masses. It's a start. From there, we have to figure out "how do I live this teaching?"

The storyteller tells us that somebody has given a cow to the ashram. So the manager reports to the Guru: "A cow has been donated."

The Guru says, "Excellent. We will all drink milk."

A couple of weeks later, the manager comes back to the Guru and says, "The person who donated the cow took the cow back."

The Guru says, "Excellent. At least we don't have to pick up cow dung."

He didn't get affected when the cow had come. And he didn't get affected when the cow was gone. He simply accepted what would happen in each case.

The storyteller says equanimity is all about the state of your mind. If you can come to the experience of equal vision in your mind, everything will be great. Whether you get married or become a sādhu, whether you live by yourself or live with others—ultimately, it boils down to the mind.

The title of the ninth chapter of the *Aṣṭāvakra Gītā* is translated as "Indifference." People in modern-day society sometimes get a little confused about this word. They wonder, "How can I live in the world and be indifferent?"

Remember the washing machine and the cloth. You don't have to become the machine. You don't have to become the water. You don't have to become the soap. You just need equanimity.

The *Bhagavad Gītā* speaks about "the place of equanimity, the place of equipoise." As I said, whether you're in your bedroom, whether you're in your living room, whether you're at the dining table, whether you're fast asleep in the middle of the night, whether you're on a stage—the same person is there twenty-four hours a day.

Sometimes people tell themselves, "Now I will be in equanimity. I want to present some teachings about equanimity, so for an hour I can manage myself." It doesn't work like that.

We had a retreat here in February for five days, during which we studied the conversation between King Janaka and Aṣṭāvakra. It was winter, so it was wonderful to snuggle up, so to speak, and think about these lofty thoughts. Hopefully, this upcoming week is not too hot and we can snuggle up in a different way and again sit with these lofty thoughts. We will have a dialogue in the morning and yoga in the afternoon. All of this is designed to bring us to the place of equanimity.

We had an all-day chant yesterday. Today is satsaṅg. We have the upcoming five-day retreat, and then the next week we have a retreat for the youth. Those are two different energies: this week will be very calm, and next week we will have the energy of youth. But all of us, no matter who we are, want to come to that place of stability, of stillness, of equanimity. That's what we seek. It is not just something we do today. What we seek has always existed, and I'm sure after we all go, it will still be there.

The scriptures tell us the Truth is that which has been, which is, and which will always be. If you can find that Truth within yourself and become established in that, then you have all that you need.

Baba Muktānanda put it very simply. He said that at the end of the day, you don't want your wife or your husband, you don't want your child or your possessions, you simply want to close your eyes and turn within. No matter how much you love them or enjoy them, you will say, "I don't want any of you now!"

In that moment, as Baba would say, there is nothing greater than the Self, or ātman, which dwells within.

THE STATE OF INDIFFERENCE

The situations that occur in our lives, as we know, are constantly changing. And yet we let ourselves get affected. We think, "Oh God!" Then we rush to Facebook and change our status. Two weeks later, we wonder, "What was I thinking?"

Satsaṅg leads us to reflect on this. Ask yourself, "Why did I get so excited last week? Why am I so upset today? I was fine before I came, and I am fine now. Did whatever happened in between really matter?"

When you have a conversation with someone, you may have a glass of water in your hand. If you are busy talking, you don't think about the glass. But after a while, you say, "Can I set this down?" The glass has become heavy because you've been holding it for so long.

Worry is like that. We all hold worry. We should just set it down.

You will ask me, "How?"

When it is a glass of water, of course that's easy. If you want to know how to set down your worries, come to the retreat for the next five days. We will have a conversation. I don't know if we'll have all the answers by Friday.

In India, in the *gurukula* tradition, a disciple lived with his Guru for a period of time. They probably had a morning session. Then they went about their day. Later, they came back together and discussed further what had been said earlier. The Guru tried to express the same teachings more clearly. The disciple tried to better understand what had been said.

So if you ask, "How do I set this down?" it is something you learn over time. One day, the realization dawns: "Ah! This is how I set it down."

Sometimes we are so constantly active in the process of our evolution, of our enlightenment, that we don't even realize we have actually left our worries behind and moved on. It is only when somebody says, "Oh, you've changed" or "You look different," that you think, "Really?"

A story is often told about two monks. One older and one younger monk are walking. They come to a stream that is overflowing.

There is a young girl there who wants to cross. So she asks the monks, "Can you carry me across?"

The older monk picks her up, carries her across, and places her on the other side.

As they continue walking, the young monk is agitated. After a while, he says, "Wait a minute! I need to ask you something. We are monks. We can't touch women. Our vows say we can't come in contact with them in any way. Yet you carried that woman across the stream."

The older monk says, "So?" He says, "I dropped her on the other side of the stream. You are still carrying her."

Situations like this occur for each and every one of us in life.

When we talk about the idea of indifference, this is the place we want to get to. We want to experience indifference on the inside. It has nothing to do with what happens on the outside. The situations we experience in the outside world are and will be what they are. What matters is the steadiness within yourself. You want to become established in that. Don't let anybody shake you. Don't let anything make you waiver.

Different traditions talk about how situations in your life can throw you into a state of upheaval. I tell people, "It is a test." We take exams at the end of our senior year in school. We give exams at the end of a course. In the same way, we have exams in life, as well.

The situations we find ourselves in test us: How much have you really learned? How much of the Truth do you actually stand for?

Around Baba Muktānanda, we had a series of courses. At the end of every course, he gave certificates. You passed if you had learned, absorbed, or imbibed whatever the teachers had taught.

Baba would say, "This certificate simply says you have done well with the material that has been presented. But the real test begins now, when you go home and you find yourself back in a situation with your family, your friends, your work. How much of all of this are you able to actually use? Then you will know whether you really passed the course. The certificate is just a piece of paper."

Thirty-five years ago, Baba Muktānanda put a garland around my neck and announced, "He will be my successor."

The whole ashram got shaken up. They thought, "What?"

Baba clarified. "I just accepted him into my university," he said. "Whether he passes or fails is up to him."

Thirty-five years later, sometimes I ask Baba in my mind, "Okay, what do you think now?" It is our own private conversation.

People come up to me and say, "Baba would be so proud of you."

I tell them, "Well, to me, what really is most important today is how I find myself being in situations. That is what is key."

As we all go through life, as we go through situations, let us find that state of equanimity, of equilibrium, and not get disturbed. That is what Aṣṭāvakra tells King Janaka: "Come to that state of indifference"—meaning don't get affected, don't let anyone throw you.

Chapter 9 of the *Aṣṭāvakra Gītā* is only a few verses. It's not that long. So we have five days in this retreat to cover eight verses. As I have said before, we don't want to have intellectual conversations. That's not what we are about. We want to understand how to live the teachings. We want to become living examples of the teachings as we go through society, through life.

One day you wake up and think "Wow!" You realize the glass you were holding has been put down. Exactly when it happened and how it happened are not important. The fact that you let go is what is important.

There's no need to preach about or vouch for what we believe in. How we live our life is, I think, in itself, the best gift we can give to ourselves and to our Guru, in gratitude for the teachings, the knowledge, and the experiences we have received.

RITUAL IS A PART OF LIFE

With great love and respect, I'd like to welcome everybody to our Sunday satsaṅg. It's supposed to be a semi-farewell satsaṅg because we go to Argentina this week, and we're back for the Thanksgiving weekend.

I thought I'd take a moment this morning to look at what we've done during this month of October. It's been a very celebratory month.

Some people came for Navarātra. Some came for Baba Muktānanda's *mahāsamādhi*. Some came for the flute concert. And most recently, we've had this week of Dīpāvalī. Some of you have been here the whole time, and others have come and gone.

In one of the homes we visited recently, the father pointed toward his teenage son and said, "I have to answer his questions, such as 'Is there a God?'" His mother was sitting next to him, and she said, "You haven't given him the traditions that we gave you, the teachings." I'm sure he felt, "Well, I've done my best."

Of course, the mind naturally wonders, "Is God for real?" So, for this past month, that's exactly what we've done—we have focused on experiencing that divinity.

First we had fifteen days of worshipping and honoring the ancestors according to the Indian tradition. In India, we call these kinds of practices *karmakand*, or rituals. Many modern-day people say, "I'm not interested in rituals."

Sages such as Ādi Śaṅkarācārya and Bhagavān Nityānanda have shown us that we don't need rituals to experience—as they themselves did—oneness with the Ultimate. But those who are still in the process of getting to that experience can't eliminate rituals completely.

Ritual is a part of life. For example, you wake up in the morning. You have your juice or tea, or whatever you prefer, and then you brush your teeth. For me, the taste of juice and toothpaste don't match, if you know what I mean. So I've resolved to do something I like better for my morning ritual. It's called oil pulling.

In the Āyurvedic tradition, you take a spoonful of sesame oil and swish it in your mouth for fifteen minutes. Just be careful that you don't swallow it and that you have a place close by where you can spit it out when you are done. Don't spit it in the sink; that's not good for the plumbing. The best is outside or in the toilet. Especially if you sniffle or have sinus issues throughout the winter, or even for all twelve months, oil pulling is beneficial.

Undigested food is what causes phlegm. Āyurveda calls it *ama*. Simply having a bowel movement doesn't mean your stomach is empty. What is left becomes stuck inside you and can stay there for years and years—much as karma and other kinds of subtle impressions do. According to Āyurveda as well as traditional Chinese medicine, most of the sicknesses we get are due to food that has not been completely digested.

I developed a sinus issue while living in the basement in Pine Bush. When we were in Haridwar in 2010, one of our swamis recommended putting warm almond oil into my nose at night before going to sleep. I told her that was a horrible idea.

But she kept at me for three or four days.

Finally I accepted the idea, because I thought that was the only way she'd leave me alone. I figured I'd have my own personal experience and then I'd tell her how horrible it was. But I liked it. Six years later, I've made it a regular practice: five drops in each nostril. It is called *nasya*. And now I can say that most of the phlegm and all the related issues I had are gone. Try it, and you'll see.

You might ask, "What does this have to do with ritual?"

Well, these are two rituals I'm introducing you to. Oil pulling is one. And the other is nasya. You can look them up.

When we do the ancestor *pūjā*, as we did at the beginning of the month, not only do we pray for our ancestors' upliftment and for good things to happen for them but we pray the same for ourselves, and for our own lives.

After that celebration finishes, we have the nine or ten days of Navarātra, during which we worship the Goddess as Mahākālī, Mahālakṣmī, and Mahāsarasvatī. These are the three aspects of the Goddess: one removes ignorance, one bestows abundance, and one gives knowledge.

The sages believed that all three aspects exist in our life. First, there is that which we need to get rid of. Then there is abundance, which is something all of us love in life. And finally, I would say, the thing we especially need more of in our lives today is wisdom.

Wisdom is not just knowing the Self, knowing the Truth. It is also knowing how to deal with basic, everyday life situations.

The word *guru* is now used across all of these situations in life. We have a management guru and a financial guru; we have this guru and that guru. But as the ancient sages told us, the one who teaches you the Truth is the Sadguru. You may have umpteen gurus, but the one who finally takes you to the knowledge of "Who am I?" is the Sadguru.

Navarātra is celebrated in March or April, as spring comes, and also in September or October, as autumn comes. One can choose to observe it during the rest of the ten months, but these are the two main times people chant the *Caṇḍī Pāṭha*, the *Lalitā Sahasranāma*, or whatever their tradition prescribes. Some people get up early in the morning, chant and pray, go to work, then come back in the evening, and again do their prayers.

Āyurveda explains that when you go from one season to the next, it is a good idea to take in less food so the body can adjust to the change. Many people fell sick in October because we had cold days, and then we had hot days. This past Thursday, we had snow. The weather changes much more rapidly now than it used to.

During Navarātra we eat less and we spend more time in japa, chanting, and meditation. This gives the body time to adjust to the change of season.

In the *Taittirīya Upaniṣad*, the Guru takes time to explain to his son—who is also his disciple—the effects of food upon the mind. What you eat determines your thoughts. It also determines how you speak. This is then translated into actions in your life.

The texts of Āyurveda discuss this at great length. The

Bhagavad Gītā also talks about it. Food is an important aspect of life that we have decided to make less important nowadays. Not only is everybody stressed these days, but everybody is trying to figure out why they are stressed. When you read about it, you see they have come up with many reasons. I say that the most important reason is that we simply don't take time for ourselves.

When people come to me and say, "I want to learn to meditate," their next question always is "And how long should I meditate?" That means they've already decided "I can only donate so much time in my day. Meditation isn't important enough to me to be flexible and open about it. Because I really don't have time."

If you don't have time, how and when will you sit? Over the years, I have seen that meditation has to be done in such a way that on some days you sit for a few moments and you feel satisfied, and on other days you need a little bit longer.

Think about what happens when you wash your clothes. The cleaner your clothes are, the less time they need in the washing machine; the dirtier they are, the longer the cycle has to run. Similarly, if your mind has taken in a lot of information throughout the day, or has gone through so much emotion, then it needs more time for cleansing. If the day has been wonderful, it needs less cleansing.

I'm talking about *truly* wonderful, not fake wonderful. I hope those of you who come regularly to satsaṅg understand what I mean by the difference between truly wonderful and fake wonderful. You have to know the difference within yourself.

Otherwise, you tell everybody, "I feel so good!" But underneath that you are thinking, "Let's sit down and talk so I can unload what really is going on."

WHERE THE GODDESS DWELLS

Every day in India has a celebration. There are celebrations for the husband, for the wife, for the son, for the daughter, for the whole family, and so on and so forth. There is no day devoid of some ceremony, of some aspect of God that is part of your life.

The way I understand it is that everybody loves to get together. But the sages decided that people couldn't just come together to eat. That couldn't be the only reason; there had to be a greater purpose. So we have celebrations so people can invite others. Of course, a major part is the food afterwards, but people can say they came for the ceremony.

During a ceremony, people are reminded that there is a God, there is Truth. If they like the priest, they have a conversation with him. They ask, "Why did you have this today?" And the conversation continues.

But these days many people just say, "Come, let's party." There is no purpose to that party other than eating, drinking, and being merry.

For example, for this celebration, we traditionally say, "*Śubha* Dīpāvalī." Meaning that we give our heartfelt greetings on the occasion of Dīpāvalī. But as the English language has crept into India, most people now say simply, "Happy Dīpāvalī." When somebody from India writes that, I write back that it is "Śubha Dīpāvalī," auspicious Dīpāvalī.

Happiness is transitory. Happiness takes place for a limited period of time. You can't really wish others happiness, because their own situation at any given time is what will determine whether they're happy or not.

The sages say, "O my mind, always have auspicious thoughts." Similarly, you can wish somebody auspiciousness. Even if you're not happy yourself, doing that helps you to come to a place of auspiciousness, to a good place within yourself.

Last night we had the pūjā to Goddess Lakṣmī as part of our Dīpāvalī festival. I shared that in India we worship Lakṣmī in eight forms.

Mahālakṣmī is her eternal nature. Gajālakṣmī is the elephant

Goddess. The elephant was a vehicle in the early days, so this refers to a way or means to get to places. Dhanalakṣmī is the Goddess of wealth, which is how most people relate to Lakṣmī.

Vijayalakṣmī or Jayalakṣmī is the Goddess of victory. Everybody wants victory in their life.

I believe in our life today we need patience and acceptance: patience to just wait out the situation, and acceptance to be at peace with it. So that is one of the forms: Dhairyalakṣmī.

Dhanyalakṣmī is the Goddess of grains. Everybody has a pantry. We have this form of the Goddess to always make sure the pantry is full.

Vidyālakṣmī is the Goddess of knowledge. The sages believed that no matter who you are, where you are, or what you are in life, knowledge is important. You must know; you must understand. This is not just school knowledge, but knowledge about how to live life and what to do with life.

Finally, Santānalakṣmī is the Goddess who oversees the ability to have children, to create progeny so this human race can continue on.

I will share a story about Lakṣmī.

Once there was an elderly man who was both rich and virtuous. In the early days in India, there were people who not only had abundant wealth but also opened their homes to everybody. They did not use their wealth selfishly. They were not miserly. What they had, they shared. The whole village felt good to have such noble people among them. One could have conversations with them and seek their advice. Sometimes they settled issues. Things in the village were taken care of.

The man in this story had thus been blessed throughout his life, as were the generations before him. But it is said that Lakṣmī is fickle. She doesn't stay with one thing. She keeps moving.

One day the man has a dream. In it, he sees a beautiful woman leaving his house. He asks her, "O Goddess, who are you? When did you come to my home, and why are you leaving?"

She says, "I am Vaibhavalakṣmī." This is yet another form

of Lakṣmī: the Goddess of grandeur and the qualities I just described that a blessed family possesses. She says, "I've been here for many generations, but now my time is up. I can't live here anymore, so I'm going to move on. But I am pleased that I was able to live here for so many generations and that I was so well used. Your family invited holy men to your home. You fed poor people. You built wells. You took care of the cows. You did a lot to uplift society. Therefore, as I leave, I want to grant you a boon. Whatever you want is what I will give you."

The man says, "I have four daughters-in-law. They manage the house. So I will consult with them and see what they want." He says, "I will get back to you."

Lakṣmī says, "Okay, I'll come back tomorrow night in your dream, and you can tell me your boon."

The next morning, the man calls his four daughters-in-law and tells them his dream.

The first one says, "Tell her to fill our safe with plenty of gold and silver and lots of wealth."

The next says, "Tell her to fill our granary."

The third agrees: "We should always have plenty of food."

The youngest daughter-in-law regularly goes to satsaṅg. She says, "Listen, if Lakṣmī wants to go, she will go. We can't stop her. Even if we ask for all of these things, they won't stay, either. Gold and silver will run out. Grain will run out. All these physical things will run out. Not only that, but our children will become full of ego, thinking, 'We come from a rich family.' They'll become lazy. They won't put forth the effort they need in life. So I feel we should ask for a blessing that will stay with us. Ask that satsaṅg and chanting happen regularly in our home. That we always honor holy men. And that there will always be love and harmony between each and every one of us, even in difficult times."

The next night the man has another dream.

Lakṣmī appears and asks, "Did you discuss the boon with your daughters-in-law?"

He says, "Yes."

She says, "So what do you want?"

He says, "O Mother Lakṣmī, if you wish to go, go with great joy. But bless us so that our home always has satsaṅg, so that holy men come to us and we're able to serve them, and so that there is great love and harmony between all of us in the family."

Lakṣmī is surprised. "What have you asked for? Because wherever there is satsaṅg, wherever holy men are served and taken care of—that is the place where Lord Nārāyaṇa dwells. And I am his wife, so wherever Nārāyaṇa dwells, I do too. Therefore, even if I wish to leave, now I cannot go. The boon you have asked for forces me to stay in this home."

The story ends here. But think about what the storyteller has tried to tell us. He says to be noble first. Because we cannot do noble actions unless we are noble. That means we have to be magnanimous ourselves. We can't be small-minded; we can't be stingy.

This is the fear people have in our society today: "Do I have enough? Can I afford to share? How much can I really share with others?"

If you look at any ancient tradition, you see the value of sharing. In fact, you only have to go back twenty years or so; that's how much things have changed. People's homes were more open, and people were more generous and willing to give and to share. Now those people might have more things in their life, but they've become more stingy. They think, "Oh, I don't know if I want to give. I don't know if I want to share. I don't know if I have enough."

But I always say, "Money just goes around: it comes and it goes. So be noble."

Here is another story.

A man arrives at a hotel. He wants to spend the night, but he wants to have a look at the room first.

The desk clerk says, "If you leave a deposit of one hundred dollars, then I'll let you see the room."

The man deposits one hundred dollars, and he goes to see

the room.

The clerk immediately takes the money and sends it to the grocer to pay his grocery bill. The grocer uses the money to pay his own bill. In this manner, the money goes from one business to another, to another, and to another. In the end, a prostitute comes back to the clerk and says, "Here's your hundred dollars."

In the meantime, the man comes back. He says, "I don't want the room." He takes the hundred dollars, puts it in his pocket, and leaves the hotel.

People like to think, "Whatever is mine is mine. And whatever is yours should become mine." That is not what this story is trying to teach us. It says, "Share! Give!" It says, "Open your pocket, open your wallet, and let what you have move, circulate."

Ultimately, we learn in life that whatever is ours will stay with us or return to us. Whatever is not ours will not stay with us no matter how well we take care of it.

You can think of it as karma. But whatever the reason may be, what does not belong with you won't stay with you.

Through the process of Navarātra, you realize that the Goddess gets rid of everything—the good, the bad, the ugly, however you want to see it—that's not yours. So we pray to her, "Take it away!"

YOU ARE NOT ALONE

Tomorrow morning we'll have our last pūjā. It will have been exactly a month, because we began on the 30th of September with the ancestor pūjā. Tomorrow's Annakuṭa pūjā is performed to the mountain of food.

The story of Annakuṭa is about Kṛṣṇa holding up Mount Govardhana. He protects all the villagers from the rain and storm sent by Lord Indra, and does it by holding the mountain over them with just his pinky.

At one point, he tells all the people who are standing around, "You want to help me? Please help."

Everybody thinks, "Why not? Let me give a hand." So they put their hand or their stick or whatever they have under the mountain.

Kṛṣṇa says, "Now that all of you are holding up the mountain, I'll just relax my pinky."

Everybody thinks, "Yeah, why not? There are so many of us—the whole village—we can handle it."

As soon as Kṛṣṇa begins to remove his pinky, the mountain starts to sink.

"No, no, no!" everybody cries. "Put your pinky back. We need you to continue to hold up the mountain!"

In our own ways, we do the same in life. We think, "You know what, God? It's okay, I can handle it. I can handle my husband. I can handle my wife. I can handle my job. I can handle my children." We say, "God, take a break. Let me show you how good I am at handling all this."

This is what we have done in society today. It's Kali Yuga, after all. We think, "Let me handle this situation. Let me show you how well I can handle this situation." All our problems arise from this.

Instead, let *all* of us handle the situation.

We began our summer like this: "Let us walk together. Let us move together. Let us come together. Let us share everything that has been given to us by God."

Now we will end our month in this way, with the understanding that "I am not alone. I should not be alone. And

I will not be alone."

As you go about your life, think about this. How can you open up your space? How can you be loving? How can you be kind? How can you be compassionate?

Remember that inviting people into your home doesn't mean you have to talk the whole time. Sometimes silence is good, also.

We try to do that here in the ashram. We have the morning chant, the noon chant, the evening chant, and we have time in between. You can just be. You can enjoy the space. You don't have to run to the next class. You don't have to run to the next event.

We have nice eight-foot-wide porches on all the buildings. Of course, it's winter now, but during the other months you can sit there. Learn to just sit.

We have made our life "run, run, run, run." When somebody says to us, "Just sit," we don't know how.

We say, "Can't I turn the television on?"

"No."

"Can't I put some music on?"

"No."

"Can't I read a book?"

"No. Just sit."

"But I want to relax."

"Yes, relax."

This is your homework for the winter. Find a place. Take your shawl or blanket or whatever you have, and sit in your own company. Sit without any of these distractions.

Look at your own thoughts. Feel your own feelings, your emotions. Ask yourself, "What is really going on?"

If you feel you need something, then I think a mirror is good. Buy a handheld mirror if you don't have one. And then have conversations.

Ask yourself, "How are you today?"

"I don't feel that good. I could be better."

"What can you do to make it better?"

You will be amazed: your questions will be answered after half an hour or forty-five minutes, or even before you put the mirror down.

Of course, that's if you know how to have a conversation. If you don't know how to do that, then take some classes. Not everybody knows how to have good, wise, uplifting conversations.

On our tour through Maryland, we met a young girl who was studying psychology. I told her, "I encourage people to study psychology, to study psychiatry." I said, "As time goes on, we're going to need more and more of that. People will need more counseling because the mental makeup in society these days is disturbed for so many reasons."

We need to take care of this. We need to make our conversations and our lives uplifting.

SALUTATIONS TO THE GODDESS

With great love and respect, I welcome you all to our Sunday satsaṅg, which we have here every Sunday, and to this festival of Caitra Navrātra, or *vasānta* Navrātra, held in the spring season. It almost looks like spring outside today.

The sages devised both these Navrātras—vasānta and *śarada*, spring and fall—at times when the weather changes. As you heard over the last two days, there was a lot of coughing here. That's what happens when nature changes outside and we don't take care of the body.

I watched a video of a talk recently by a doctor who had lost his son to a vitamin deficiency. He said, "As a doctor, I wasn't able to help him, because we only know what to do after sickness arises." He didn't talk about any of the traditional ways of medicine, but he said, "We are taught in medical school to look only at disease; instead, we should be looking at how to attain optimal health."

What he said reminded me of a story Baba Muktānanda used to tell.

A man goes to Mullah Nasruddin and says—like some of you here—"I have a cold and a cough."

Nasruddin says, "Go home and bathe for the next seven days with cold water. And then come back."

The man says, "I will have pneumonia!"

Nasruddin says, "Exactly. I have a treatment for pneumonia. But for this kind of basic, simple cold or cough, there is nothing I can give you."

When we follow the tradition of Navrātra in India, my doctor gives me a little shot of neem juice. For the ten days of Navrātra, every morning we take this bitter drink. Many of you in the West have now heard of neem and its beneficial medicinal effects.

On Tuesday, Lavarji invoked the Goddess in this vessel of water. Water is the best conductor in nature. Just put your foot in some water and hold onto an electric wire, and you'll see. The sages realized that water is the best way to invoke energy, so they taught priests that this is what they should use to gather energy.

When you invite a God or a Goddess, that deity comes with his or her retinue.

In the ancient tradition, no matter where you were from, you never sailed alone, you were never allowed to go somewhere alone. In India, when we were young, we would look at the elders who wanted someone to go with us, and say, "I don't want him. I can go alone, I'm old enough now. I'm not a baby, what will he do?"

But the elders would say, "No, it's okay, just take him along."

Sometimes we would figure out how to dump the person. But if he was smart or had been dumped before, he also knew what tricks we were up to. So we didn't go alone. I see the elders laughing now; they can relate to all of this.

When Lavarji invokes the deity, it's the same thing. He invites the universal Consciousness, and she comes with her many attendants. This includes the nine planets and Lord Gaṇeśa and the fifty-six beings, and so on and so forth.

In Magod, usually whenever we traveled, somebody would ask me, "Who's going to be coming with you?"

I said, "Well, whoever is around at the time and I feel is appropriate can come." Simple, right?

But one day I was told, "You can't choose anymore."

I said, "Why?"

They said, "Because you will leave some out."

I said, "Okay, whoever is going to come along, first of all, has to be useful." It's not that those who come are there just to occupy space, eat, and make merry. Everyone who comes on a tour has to fulfill a purpose. They can play the harmonium or the drums or the cymbals, or sing, or do pūjā, or cook, or drive, or clean."

I said, "Of the many sevās on the tour—whatever role needs to be played, or whatever role has been given to you—I don't want to worry, 'Is that job being fulfilled or not?' I just want to know that it's happening from early morning, through the day, or at night."

Each one of us, I believe, in our life, has this kind of role, or purpose. The way I think of it, that role becomes our connection to divinity, to Consciousness, to Truth.

The question arises in each one's mind: "What is it that I must do? What should I do to constantly maintain this connection?"

Connection does not happen automatically. It happens because of the effort that each and every one of us puts forth. And the effort we put forth bears fruit.

We worshipped the Goddess just now by reciting thirteen chapters of the *Caṇḍī Pāṭha*. If you have your book, or if you study it when you go home, you will read the refrain

yā devī sarva-bhūteṣu,
namas-tasyai, namas-tasyai,
namas-tasyai namo namaḥ.

You understand, "In all of these various forms in which you exist within me"—whether man or woman, it doesn't matter—"I offer my salutations, I offer my salutations, I offer my salutations to you."

There is a verse I love that is attributed to Abhinavagupta. He says, "O Goddess, whatever thoughts arise in my mind, whatever forms I see in this world, are nothing but an expression of your own form. I have darśan of you through all of these forms. All the activities that take place in this world are nothing but the expression of your various forms; therefore, everything should be considered as pūjā, as worship."

Each of us must bring our mind to the place where it constantly maintains that connection, maintains that oneness.

WHAT ARE YOU GOING TO OFFER?

When we traveled through Australia in 2010, everywhere I went, I shared that we have to be like milk. One fear you have when you have milk is that if a drop of lemon falls into the container of milk, all the milk will be spoiled. It will become curdled. Of course, whether that is a good thing or not depends on if you like cheese.

In the community we are in, or the world we are in, we definitely don't want to be that drop of lemon. We can decide later whether we can become milk, but let's first work on making sure that "I will not be that drop of lemon juice." I think we can begin there.

We want this sweetness, this kindness, this love, this compassion to spread.

When we had our retreat this past year, the T-shirt that was given out said, "An army of lovers can change the world." This came from something I heard Baba say in 1978 in Oakland, California. He said, "If I had an army of lovers…" So we got rid of the "If I had" and just wrote "An army of lovers can change the world." That idea has to be planted so it can happen. And we must do it.

Recently I read a little story about a girl who was going around selling milk. In the old days, one used to get a bottle of milk or a can of milk delivered at one's door. In India, we still have people who come around on their bicycle or motorcycle with containers of milk, and they measure out a quarter of a liter or half a liter or one liter.

So this girl is selling milk, and a boy comes with his bottle. She just pours the milk into it. She doesn't measure a quarter or a half of a liter, or a liter; she just pours the milk.

An observer who is standing nearby asks his friend, "Why didn't she first measure the milk?"

The friend says, "Because that's the boy she loves." In other words, because she loves him, there is no reason to measure what she gives him; she gives unconditionally, without measurement.

A sādhu is also standing there. He listens to these friends

talking, and he says to himself, "Each day I sit here and repeat, '*Oṁ Namaḥ Śivāya, Oṁ Namaḥ Śivāya, Oṁ Namaḥ Śivāya.*' And then I think, 'Oh my God, how many more repetitions do I have to do?'"

This is what we do. We think, "I have to do one *mālā*." Or "I have to do five." Or "I have to do eleven." Each one of us has our method. For example, we say, "I'm doing eleven mālās for you, Baba. Look, watch me."

And then we question: "One mālā is only worth half a liter of milk?"—a liter of milk meaning grains of compassion, of deliverance. We think, "No, one mālā should be worth at least one liter of milk."

The sādhu realizes, "That girl loves that boy and gives him milk without measuring, but I claim to love God and I am measuring each mantra I offer. I am bargaining with God. I am not giving unconditionally."

I would like to end by saying, "Think about this: what good can I offer society?"

Society is first of all your own family—your parents, husband, wife, brother, sister, mother, father, and so on. We all have different roles, or places, in society, in life. After you have the people you live with every day, you have those who are a little bit further outside. You have your coworkers. You have your regular, everyday contacts. And then you have your once-in-a-while contacts.

Here we have our once-a-year visitors. They know, "I only come here for this day, or this program and that program. I won't see you again until next year on this day." At least there's some clarity.

So think about what you can do, what you can offer. You can look it up on the Internet to get some ideas.

Each society has its own way to help others. It could be "Let's go somewhere and feed or clothe people." Or you could choose to do something different. For example, organize a party.

A long time ago there was a girl in Australia who was in

college and had just gotten associated with Shanti Mandir. For some occasion, she organized a sit-down dinner, like we do in the ashram. In front of everybody, she put an envelope that contained a gift certificate for the eye camp we hold near Haridwar. She told her friends, "I don't want a gift for myself. I don't need one more thing, but if you wish to give something, this is something you can do."

I'm not going to tell you what you should do or must do; I'm just suggesting something you can think about. That's part of my job—to provoke thought. And I'll leave it at that.

Of course, this thought is provoked within myself, as well. Each day when I wake up, I think, "Okay, what are we going to do today?"

When we have a five-day or a seven-day or a ten-day retreat, people come with their notebooks and pens and I have to tell them, "The Self is within you." I wonder, "How do I tell this differently today?" This message is already written in the *Upaniṣads*. It's already in the *Bhagavad Gītā*. I wonder how I can say it now so they go home today feeling, "Wow! That was something new."

It's not new. It is that which has always been.

Today, hopefully you remember: Never travel alone. Always take somebody with you. Remain connected to God. Be milk. If anybody wants to be lemon juice, it's okay; we can handle you, too. And don't measure, just give.

This is the vibration, this is the energy, this is the Consciousness we want to carry with us as we go through life.

I invite you to come again this summer. Spend a weekend, a few days, a few weeks, a few months, a few years, a few lifetimes: the choice is yours.

THE WORLD IS AS YOU SEE IT

With great love and respect, I welcome you to our Intensive here. As everybody came up for darśan at the end of the program last night, it was great to see all of the smiling faces.

And it was especially joyous to see the young people here. Normally teenagers think that an event like this is boring. They wonder, "What are my parents doing?"

You can tell them that many adults feel the same way, even at the age they are now. It takes a long time to come to an understanding about this path.

Earlier this month, we were in Northern California in a retreat like this. An American man gave me a quote. In it, the monk says, "Looking for serenity, you have come to the monastery." For us, this Intensive is our monastery today. And then the monk says, "Looking for serenity, I am leaving the monastery."

People of the world come to a monastery to become silent. But the monk, who has been living in the monastery for a long time, tortured by his own mind, is leaving that monastery. He is running away from the silence.

Baba Muktānanda always said, "The mind is the cause of our bondage, and the mind is the cause of our liberation." He illustrated this through a story about a king who builds a palace of mirrors.

By accident, a dog walks into that palace of mirrors. Everywhere the dog looks, he sees another dog. So he begins to growl.

The dog in the mirror growls back.

Then the first dog shows his teeth.

And the dog in the mirror also shows his teeth.

The first dog barks.

And the dog in the mirror barks back.

Everywhere the dog turns, he sees another dog growling, another dog barking, another dog showing its teeth. So he becomes filled with fear, and he falls to the floor and dies.

A sage walks into that same palace of mirrors. He looks at all the various forms in the mirrors, and he knows each is his own reflection. He appreciates being able to see so many different forms of himself.

What is the difference between the dog and the sage? When you don't perceive the oneness in everything, your mind becomes filled with fear. When your mind realizes that all of this is simply a manifestation of the same Consciousness, it begins to enjoy looking at all of it.

The whole purpose of meditation—and of understanding this knowledge—is to come to a place of oneness, to bring the mind to a place of quiet. That is what our day today is about.

Like the monk, you will leave this monastery tomorrow. But hopefully by the time you do, you'll have attained some peace and quiet within yourself.

Whenever we come together like this, each person has made the decision to take the time for spiritual practice. Somewhere within yourself there is a desire to know something. You may not understand everything by the end of the weekend, but a little understanding of the question "Who am I?" can come about.

Many things happen in our lives. How we understand these things depends on the state of our mind. The sage says, "The world is as you see it." If you see the world as a wonderful place, it is a wonderful place. If you see it as a miserable place, you will find it is full of misery.

What the sage is saying is that the only place that needs fixing is the mind. Each of us is tortured by nothing else and no one else except our own mind.

As you study the scriptures, you realize that they focus upon perception. Let's take an example from the early days, when people had two or three old-fashioned landlines in the house. Imagine you are sitting at home, waiting for a phone call you were supposed to get at 9 a.m. That time has come and gone.

You begin to think, "Well, that person never liked me." And you think, "I don't love that person anyway."

You're sitting on your bed with these thoughts when your mother walks into the room and asks, "What is going on?"

You say, “I was expecting a call at 9 a.m. It’s almost nine thirty, and the phone hasn’t rung.”

Your mother says, “Let me check the phones.” So she goes into the other room and sees that one phone is off the hook. As soon as she puts it back on, the phone rings.

Your friend says, “I’ve been calling you for the last thirty minutes, and the phone has been busy.”

You don’t say anything about all the thoughts you had for the last thirty minutes, because all of a sudden your perception has changed completely. Those thirty minutes of perception were all in your imagination. Now you realize there was no need to create any of those thoughts.

The sages tell us that we are what we think.

Good, uplifting thoughts make us free. Thoughts like those from the thirty minutes bind us. They upset us and make us angry. They take us to the wrong places within ourselves. But with just a little light, a little illumination, the problem is gone. We have to remember to put the phone back on the hook, and everything will be fine.

Yoga brings about a shift in the way we see this world. Through the process of meditation, we make a shift in our mind’s perception. The mind can focus upon anything, but we want it to focus upon something worthy.

Instead of focusing on unworthy ideas or concepts, the process of spiritual practice, of sādhanā, reminds us again and again, “O my mind, have noble thoughts.”

Whether you are a little child, a teenager, a middle-aged person, or a person in the elder years, you can tell your mind, “Have noble thoughts.”

As the mind begins to have noble thoughts, this world also becomes wonderful. The world doesn’t change. Nothing changes on the outside. The change is in your own mind.

WHERE DID YOU PUT YOUR UMBRELLA?

It takes a long time to understand the mind.

A student stays in a monastery for twelve years. At the end of twelve years, he thinks it is time for him to progress to the next level. So he asks his teacher in the monastery where he should go.

The teacher advises him to go to a particular monastery where he will find a master who is at the next level.

On his way there, it is raining, as it was here last night. When he arrives at the second monastery, he places his umbrella outside the door and goes in.

The new teacher asks him, “On which side of the door did you leave your umbrella: left or right?”

The student says, “I don’t know.”

The teacher says, “Then go back to your first teacher. If you don’t even remember whether you placed your umbrella on the left or the right, how will you know where you have placed your mind?”

We tend to think of learning yoga and meditation in a class, like what we are doing right now. But great teachers, such as Baba Muktānanda, give us a little teaching and then tell us, “Now sit with it.” Every so often, they ask us a question: “Where did you place the umbrella?”

We think, “Is it important where I placed the umbrella?” But to them, there is nothing that is less important, and nothing that is more important. Everything is important when it comes to where we place our mind.

So this weekend, observe your mind. None of us is tortured by anything besides the mind. Learn to place your mind correctly. Whether it’s to the left, right, or center doesn’t matter; find the place that’s most appropriate in your life.

Let your mind become quiet. Let it become peaceful. Allow the gentleness that is within you to come forth. Allow yourself to become still. Focus your mind.

You may still have some thoughts, but those thoughts won’t torture or even worry you when you have become quiet and peaceful within yourself.

Learn to smile with the joy that dwells within. You don't need to wait for a special moment for something to happen. Now is the moment.

In the *Aṣṭāvakra Gītā*, the sage Aṣṭāvakra talks about bondage and freedom. He holds a long conversation with King Janaka, who asks, "Why is it that I find myself far away from the Self?"

The sage explains that the mind is always rushing out. It is grazing among the world of objects. It is running wild among these objects, rejecting things it feels are not conducive and pursuing things it imagines to be conducive. It thinks those things will bring it happiness.

The mind is both hunting after objects and being hunted itself. It is constantly constructing and destroying, loving and fighting. From the time it is inside the womb of the mother till the time it dies, the mind—and ego—is constantly struggling. It's always suffering. This, the sage says, is bondage.

The *Upaniṣads* describe bondage with one word: mine. Every time the mind thinks, "Mine, mine, mine," that is bondage. Every time the mind thinks, "Not mine," that is freedom.

The sage tells us that, throughout life, we must live with the awareness that nothing is really mine. Let the mind not grieve, accept, or reject. Let it not feel happy or sad. Doing that will only lead to bondage. The sage Aṣṭāvakra tells Janaka to come to this place within himself.

The *Yoga Vāsiṣṭha* says that the reduction of thoughts is freedom. When the mind stops desiring, that is freedom.

Similarly, Patañjali tells us that yoga is the cessation of all the modifications of thought.

The experience of stillness, of one-pointedness, is the result of a reduction in the thought process. You teach the mind to become detached. You want to come to a place where you are not operating from a sense of ego. Stop accepting and rejecting, and just allow yourself to be in a place of play. Look at everything as nothing but a play of Consciousness.

The sages remind us again and again that what we seek

cannot be found outside. It is found within us. It is found within when all the various desires that arise through the mind have dried up. When those desires have been conquered, the whole cycle of thoughts ceases. And when thoughts cease, the mind becomes quiet. This is the state of freedom.

The *Bhagavad Gītā* says, "An individual who has conquered his mind has come to live in perfect equanimity in all conditions of life, in all relationships. He indeed rests in the Absolute."

As you move about today—as you pick up something, as you place something down, as you open and close doors—allow yourself to be more conscious. We perform a lot of actions, but many are performed without awareness. What we want to do is bring about greater awareness of where our mind is, so our actions can be performed with understanding.

Just as the teacher asked, "Where did you place the umbrella?" as you go about your activities today, be conscious of all that you are doing.

A seeker is always seeking knowledge, seeking wisdom. A seeker is always contemplating. A seeker wants his mind to always be doing uplifting work, to constantly use discrimination. The mind is trying to understand what is happening in life, and we want to slowly bring it to the place where it is performing good thoughts, and through good thoughts, good actions.

THE MIND'S TRUE NATURE

The purpose of repetition of the mantra is to bring the mind to contemplate its own true nature. Normally, as the sage said, the mind is running outside into the objects of this world. Instead, we want that mind to go inside and contemplate its true nature.

The mantra we use in meditation is *Haṁsa*. *Haṁ* is "I am" and *sa* is "That." As you repeat the mantra, your mind comes to the awareness and the understanding of "I am That," or I am the divine Self.

Instead of being worried about all the various things it worries about, the mind begins to contemplate its true nature. Take your mind away from the body, away from all the various thoughts you always have. Let it come to sit in the awareness of "I am That."

A conscious effort has to be put forth by each and every one of us to, first of all, be comfortable inside our own body. Then, when you are comfortable within your own body, slowly become aware of your breathing, of the breath.

When your breathing becomes even, allow yourself to focus upon *Haṁsa*. As the breath goes in, *Haṁ*; as the breath goes out, *sa*. Let the mind become free of all dualities, of all sense of separation, of all the various things that torture you during a normal day. Bring it to a place of peace.

The *Upaniṣads* tell us that our basic nature is ānanda, bliss. If our nature is bliss, let us experience and feel that.

Throughout this day, let us become quiet. Let us become still. Let us become focused. Let us develop our own clarity. Let us become steady. Let us dwell within, with our own Self. We want that by the end of the day, we have all come closer to that divinity, that Truth, that Self, that dwells within us.

May we all recognize the Self. May we find satisfaction. May we find contentment. May we experience peace within our own being. And as we become peaceful and contented, and our minds become quiet, may we also experience oneness.

It's just a matter of a few hours. Around five o'clock, you will have the choice whether you want to continue to remain in that quiet and stillness or go back to what you are used to. At least until five o'clock, give yourself permission to have a day of stillness, a day of quietude.

Just trust and be at peace in your own being. Thoughts will arise, desires will arise, doubts will arise, but allow yourself to remain quiet. The choice really is our own. We have to teach ourselves to live this kind of life, to do all our activities from that place of stillness.

DOWN THE CHIMNEY

With great respect and love, you are welcome to the Intensive here this afternoon.

Our topic today is liberation. Over the years, there's been much discussion about what everyone thinks liberation might be. It's easy to have a conceptual idea of liberation.

A young man in his mid-twenties knocks on the door of a renowned Guru and says, "I've come to you because I wish to study the *Vedas*."

The Guru asks him, "Do you know Sanskrit?"

He says no.

"Have you studied any Indian philosophy?"

He says, "No, I haven't, but I just finished my doctoral dissertation at Harvard on Socratic logic. To round off my education, I want to add a little study of the *Vedas*."

The Guru says, "I doubt you're ready to study the *Vedas*, because that is the deepest form of knowledge. Yet if you wish, I'm willing to test you in logic. If you pass, then I will teach you the *Vedas*."

The young man agrees.

So the Guru holds up two fingers and says, "Two men come down a chimney. One comes out with a dirty face, and the other comes out with a clean face. Which one washes his face?"

The young man stares at the Guru and says, "Is this really a test of logic?"

The Guru says, "Yes."

The fellow says confidently, "The one with the dirty face washes his face."

The Guru says, "Wrong. The one with the clean face washes his face. Examine the logic. The one with the dirty face looks at the one with the clean face, and the one with the clean face looks at the one with the dirty face."

The young man says, "Very clever. Please give me another test."

The Guru holds up two fingers and says, "Two men come down a chimney. One comes out with a clean face, and the other comes out with a dirty face. Which one washes his face?"

The young man says, "We already established that. The one with the clean face washes his face."

The Guru says, "Wrong. Examine the logic. The one with the dirty face looks at the one with the clean face and thinks, 'His face is clean.' The one with the clean face looks at the one with the dirty face and thinks, 'His face is dirty.' So the one with the clean face washes his face. And when the one with the dirty face sees the clean one wash his face, he also washes his face. So each one washes his face."

The young man says, "Well, I didn't think of that. It's shocking that I could make an error in logic. Test me again."

The Guru holds up two fingers and says the same thing: "Two men come down a chimney. One comes out with a clean face, and the other comes out with a dirty face. Which one washes his face?"

The young man says, "Each one washes his face."

The Guru says, "Wrong. Neither of them washes his face. Examine the logic. The one with the dirty face looks at the one with the clean face and thinks, 'His face is clean.' The one with the clean face looks at the one with the dirty face and thinks, 'His face is dirty.' But when the one with the clean face sees that the one with the dirty face doesn't wash his face, he also doesn't wash his face. So neither one washes his face."

The young man is desperate. He says, "I'm qualified to study the *Vedas*. Just give me one more test."

So the Guru again holds up two fingers and repeats the same question. "Two men come down the chimney. One comes out with a clean face, and the other comes out with a dirty face. Which one washes his face?"

The young man says, "Neither one washes his face."

The Guru again says, "Wrong." He says, "How can two people come down a chimney, and one have a clean face while the other has a dirty face? That means the logic that you've been trying to use all this time to figure this out is nonsense. The whole question is based on foolishness. If you spend your whole life trying to answer foolish questions, your answers will be foolish too."

May we all have the wisdom to ask and answer only wise questions.

Here is another story. There was a great sage in Maharashtra called Eknāth Mahārāj. His son goes to Varanasi to study and then comes back after having studied. He tells his father, "You know, you've been teaching for a long time. You must be tired. Your audience must also be bored with the same teachings. So let me teach in your place."

Eknāth says, "Okay."

So the son speaks to his father's followers. On the first day, there is a huge crowd, and everybody is excited that the young man has come back from Varanasi to teach. But each day, the crowd grows thinner. Fewer and fewer people come.

Finally Eknāth asks somebody, "Why have people stopped attending?"

The person says, "Your son teaches, '*Ahaṁ Brahmāsmi*. I am the Absolute. I am the Truth.' That we know already. It's nothing new. We liked the way you expressed the teachings."

So often, many of us get caught in words. I remember once someone asked Baba about such-and-such a swami who had written a great book. He asked Baba, "Do you think that swami is a *siddha*?"

Baba simply said, "Siddhas don't have time to do research."

BE THAT DROP OF HONEY

The important thing is to remember that life is a play; it's an illusion. We tend to forget that.

For example, imagine a room. There's a ball in that room, and each of us has a mallet. Each one of us hits the ball with the mallet when it comes to us.

There is also a little opening underneath the door in that room. When it gets to that little opening, the ball goes out.

The ball represents the mind, or the soul, that is living inside the body. The mallet is all of us, with our illusions, who are hitting the ball.

When the final hit throws the ball out of the room—which is like the soul leaving the body—you have to ask yourself: How was it hit? What was the speed at which it went? What was the impact? What was the cause? What were all the various things it took with it?

After it leaves that room, the ball, or soul, finds a new room, which is a new body, and it enters there. It takes with it all our malleable—or we could say mallet-able—impressions. There, the next play starts up again, in a new situation. And you have to ask: How do I deal with the impressions I have brought with me from the first room?

This is the philosophy of karma. The Indian scriptures don't discuss sin. Rather, they speak about the possibility of higher thinking.

The sages tell us that life is like a Ferris wheel. A Ferris wheel goes around; when you ride on it, you go up and then down. I haven't been on one for a long time, but you get on it and you go up and then you come down, and you go up and you come down. And then you get off, and somebody else gets in your seat. They go up, and they come down.

Sometimes you get excited. Your friend says, "Let's go again!" So you get in a different seat. You go up, you go down. You get on the Ferris wheel and you get off the Ferris wheel just as you enter the body and you leave the body.

The world keeps going around and around and around. Some days it feels like you're up, you are elevated, you are in an altered state of consciousness.

Baba often said the biggest mistake we can make is to think, "I am incapable." This is what happens to many of us: we don't even begin something we want to do, because we think, "I don't know if I'll make it."

If we go back to the story I began with about logic, you could say, "Well, if that's the case, then why do I even want to study?"

If you don't study, then you won't know whatever you want to know. If you don't make the effort, your study won't bear fruit.

The philosophy of Kashmir Shaivism talks about knowledge of two kinds. One is knowledge you gain through studying with a Guru, a teacher; the second involves taking that knowledge into life and applying it.

You can't just live life without knowledge. And you can't just have knowledge without bringing it into your life.

Swami Chinmayānanda said it takes three thousand lifetimes to even begin the study of scriptures. I say, "Okay, forget about the three thousand lifetimes. At least this lifetime, now that you are living, you can think about what you are doing."

Ask yourself, "What will I do to make my life peaceful and blissful?"

The example I often use is that there is a drop of honey on the counter. No text message has been sent out, yet all the flies, ants, and bees come to that drop of honey.

Think about it. I ask myself this often: how does this network of life work such that a drop of sugar on the counter—just a granule of sugar, a single drop of honey—is enough to attract the flies, the ants, the bees, and whatever else? Somehow they know to come there, sometimes even through a screened-in window. How do they make it inside?

When I read the scriptures, I think, "Okay. Each of us should try to be that drop of honey on the counter." I don't mean literally on a physical kitchen counter but on the counter of life. How can each of us be so that people are naturally drawn to us?

The poet-saint Chokhamela tells us that he is hugging Lord Viṭṭhal. He describes hundreds of thousands of people in the crowd who are singing the name of God. They are all lost in chanting and dancing. And in their midst Chokhamela says he is embracing God.

If you're a normal, logical person standing outside that crowd and looking at them, they may seem like madmen and women. But they're mad with love, mad with feeling. They are like a million drops of honey. At least, we can say there are that many drops of honey around the earth.

I ask myself, "Okay, what are the qualities that transform pollen into honey?"

There's a process. And if we are all pollen, then we have to ask, "How do I change myself? What is the method?"

Of course, you can go to different people who love this process of making honey. We know an elderly gentleman in Pine Bush who has six or eight hives. You can spend an hour with him—that's a minimum—and he will explain how the bees come, how the bees go, how he sends them away, what he does, and how they live in the winter.

This process is happening in nature. But then you think, "Okay, now I have to translate this to myself. I am the pollen. I am the bee. I am everything." And you realize there's nothing on the outside that's going to convert you from being "non-honey" into being honey. You have to do it yourself.

Somehow, the way human beings are designed, we always look outside. We don't realize we need to look within.

Therefore, when Swami Chinmayānanda says three thousand lifetimes, it's not actually so much time.

The way I see it is that it is like going to a big, thick tree trunk and sawing it. Suppose you only have a blunt saw or maybe only a blunt knife. Therefore, you are sitting there for three thousand lifetimes or six thousand lifetimes, or maybe even six hundred thousand lifetimes. Your knife is so blunt that it's not actually cutting. You imagine that it's cutting, but it's not really cutting.

Of course, you could get a sharper knife and still be sitting there and still have a lot of arrogance, and a lot of all the stuff that comes with that.

THE VEIL OF ILLUSION

During the summer, I talked about the story of Gulliver. He washed up onto the island, and he was knocked unconscious. As he's lying there, the Lilliputians, the little pygmy people, are running around and tying this big man down.

When he becomes conscious, Gulliver realizes he has been tied down. So he tells the little people, "If you let me loose, I'll help you win the island next door."

The scriptures tell us five things tie us down: desire, anger, greed, delusion, and envy.

You could say there are sub-ropes too. For example, anger can lead to frustration. Anger can lead to upset.

The delusion we live in is thinking that these ropes are no longer tying us up, and therefore we are free. Yet the most important rope remains: the veil of illusion rope remains. There is a big difference between thinking, "I am free" and actually being free.

Baba Muktānanda used to say that a normal ego is better than a spiritual ego because at least a normal ego is identifiable. It knows it is tied up. But a spiritual person thinks, "I am spiritual. I've gotten rid of almost all the ropes. I only have this veil of illusion left, so I am better, I am higher, I am greater."

We think it is easy to get rid of these ropes, but really it's not so easy.

At the same time, it's not a process to see as upsetting. As I travel, I meet people around the world who think sādhanā is painful, upsetting, something to fear. For me, it's about joy. It's about experiencing the joy that dwells within you. Yes, it may feel painful to let go, to get rid of something. But the ultimate feeling of becoming free is joyful.

The *Upaniṣads* give a list of things that happen to a person who rises above or goes beyond all the things of this world. They say, "He treats others with respect, regardless of how others treat him."

In other words, you are nice to others not because they are nice but because you are.

And the *Upaniṣads* say about such a person, "When confronted by an angry person, he does not return anger but instead replies with soft and kind words." Such a person is "comfortable with a begging bowl at the foot of a tree, in tattered robes, whether in a village or the city. He doesn't care for all the religious markings. He is humble and high-spirited. He has a clear and steady mind. He is straightforward, compassionate, patient, indifferent, and courageous."

I often use the example of a clear glass of water. Water on its own has no color. Generally, water doesn't have any taste. So, that's how a human being should be too. He should be clear.

Yet we go through all of these emotions, and these emotions color us. Then people say, "He's always angry." "She always wants something." "He's always envious." "She is greedy."

The last thing that leaves us is the veil of illusion. The other ropes fall away one by one, yet the veil of illusion stays with us for a long time.

I'll end with a story. A man sees what appears to be a rug flowing down the river. He wants to have it, so he jumps into the water.

A friend is standing on the bank. As he watches the man being carried away, he calls out, "Come back!"

The man says, "It's not a rug. It's a bear!"

The friend says, "Then let go."

The man says, "I have, but it has not."

This happens to many of us in the river of life. Somehow we get caught. We want to let go, and we even imagine that we have let go, but it carries us. We think we have conquered it, yet it surfaces again and again. Only when we finally shake it off, can we say, "That's it; done," and be free.

THE DAY OF THE GURU

With great respect and love, I would like to welcome everyone here this morning. Today is the full moon of this month of July. All over the world, yesterday and today, many people have celebrated Guru Pūrṇimā.

Today we also celebrate thirty years of the existence of Shanti Mandir. Thirty years ago, we started doing this. For me, actually, it's been fifty-six years of celebrating Guru Pūrṇimā.

Now we have a small place, half an acre, in Ganeshpuri, that someone donated. On this day of Guru Pūrṇimā, we are there for the first time. I think we have one bedroom, a living room, a verandah, a kitchen, and a bathroom—it depends on how you add up the rooms.

To clarify what some of us were talking about earlier, the ashram Bhagavān Nityānanda gave Baba Muktānanda in Ganeshpuri was the front portion of that property. Many people who came after 1970 never saw the original building, which had an L-shaped meditation hall and three rooms that became what is today the Nityānanda Temple.

When you walked in the gate, there was a parijata tree. It was very simple. In the hall, there was a picture of Bhagavān similar to—or maybe the same one as—the picture that's up in Turiya Mandir now. And there was Bhagavān's statue.

Baba originally had that statue made for the samādhi shrine in Ganeshpuri. But the main trustee there did not want a gift from Swami Muktānanda. Baba was, we could say, positive aggressive. I've heard people talk in these last few years about being passive aggressive, and I don't think that's the right word. Positive aggressive fits better. So, when the temple trustees decided not to take that statue, Baba said to his man Friday—whom some of you may remember, Venkappa—"Okay, let's build a temple at the ashram."

Baba wasn't just positive aggressive, he was doubly positive and doubly aggressive. The original three rooms were taken down, and within three and a half months, a whole new building had been built. This was in 1970, while Baba was away on his first world tour. For those of you who think India is backwards today, imagine doing all that in three and a half months!

What had been the meditation room became Baba's room. He lived there for a short time, and later it became his shrine. In the meantime, they built him a newer house in the back, which he moved into.

Baba always said, "See God in each other. God dwells within you as you."

Sometimes you may forget to see God in each other. You think, "Well, they just don't see the God in me yet, and I don't see the God in them yet either."

Another thing Baba said was "The belief that anything other than love will end suffering is the cause of suffering."

When we think about Baba's messages, we realize that one of the words common to many of them is *love*. The exact word *love* doesn't exist in the Indian scriptures. Strange, isn't it? I guess the sages thought, "Love as people think of it is temporary, fleeting, dependent, so why talk about love? Let's talk about *ānanda*." Ānanda means, we could say, love-bliss.

Today, as we celebrate Guru Pūrṇimā, we think of ānanda.

When we lived in Pine Bush for three years, there was a devotee who drove a huge station wagon. One day, it drove itself into a ditch, and then she got a little car.

I have an interest in cars and I know the brands, models, technical details, and so on. So when this woman told me about the Ford she bought, I said, "There's no such car, no such model of Ford."

She said, "Come, look."

So I went with her. When I saw the car, I said, "Wow, I've never seen this model before!" We drove it, and the mechanic said it was good, and she bought it. But then, everywhere we went on the freeway, guess what I saw? Not her car, but that particular model of Ford.

When it comes to God, or to the Guru, I think something similar can happen. You've never heard of the Guru. You've never seen the Guru. You've never even thought about the Guru. Then, all of a sudden, somebody puts the Guru in front of you, or you run into the Guru. And then, as the poet-saint says, "Wherever I look, I only see You."

In India, one can buy the statues of deities from an artist who makes them.

The artist says, "One lakh rupees."

You say, "No, 65,000."

A deal is finally struck somewhere around 85,000 or 90,000.

You buy the statue and take it home. Then you sit in front of the statue and say to the deity, "I'm buying a lotto ticket this week. It's worth so many hundreds of millions."

When you bought that statue, you were negotiating with the artist for a few thousand rupees, but now you're asking the deity for millions and billions. This is how we treat love—as this kind of deal.

As we celebrate this day of the Guru, we have to ask ourselves some serious and sincere questions: What am I really doing? What is really going on? And where is it that I am headed?

MAY I NEVER FORGET YOU

These fifty-six years of life have been wonderful. That doesn't mean they have been without challenges, with no turbulence. The seat belt has been on. Sometimes one feels that the pilot has been doing acrobatics when he shouldn't be. Then he says, "Trust me."

Many years ago, someone gave me a book somebody had given him. He said, "I don't understand the language. I hope you can read it." It was in Marathi, and the author is sharing the teachings of Bhagavān Nityānanda. I just love the title: *May I Never Forget You.* Or *May You Never Be Forgotten.* I often think simply of this title, and I tell my mind, "May you never, even for a few moments or seconds, forget the Guru, forget grace."

We should forever be grateful for all that we have received in life.

In Magod, we had a student who was with us for almost twelve years. He has a brilliant mind. He graduated and has now gone off to study Sanskrit grammar with a different teacher.

A devotee who was visiting the ashram a few years ago asked this student, "How are you?"

The student was probably sixteen or seventeen at the time. He looked at the devotee and said, "Great. How else should one be in the ashram?"

Somebody who overheard this conversation reported it to me, and I said, "Excellent." I was impressed that somebody who was only about sixteen knew that the question "How are you?" is invalid in the ashram, where one lives in the balloon of grace.

That is gratitude. A person who experiences gratitude becomes content. His mind becomes cheerful. In his life, there is no misery, no suffering. In such a person, the *buddhi*, the intellect, moves away from wrong thinking and wrong doing and becomes established in the upliftment of oneself. When the mind no longer goes down, but simply rises, we experience *prasād*, a blessing. We experience grace.

We tend to think of struggle as trouble. But our scriptures tell us that struggle is not trouble. Struggle is simply the polishing of the individual so he can shine.

People come to the ashram and say, "Why don't you have television?"

I say, "It's not necessary." Really, it's not.

Come and visit us. We have lots of ideas we can share with you. And you can entertain yourself as well. You can laugh. You can cry. Terrifying things won't happen to you here, because if you chant, meditate, and have satsaṅg, the mind stays positive and only thinks uplifting things.

Somebody who was part of an ashram from a very young age told me that some bad things had happened to her in life. Of course that can happen. She said, "You know, many people think that one bad thing makes the whole thing bad, or wrong."

In English, there's a saying: "Don't throw out the baby with the bath water." I think those of us associated with an ashram, a temple, or a path should always remember this. After all, we are human. Whether we live out in the world or live in the ashram, we are the same person. If a person does stuff out there, he's going to do that same stuff here in the ashram too.

This person who had the bad thing happen gave an example. In the ashram we serve khichdi, which is made of rice and lentils, for dinner on Saturday nights. Those who love khichdi come to the ashram on Saturday night. She said, "Imagine that khichdi has been laced with poison. The khichdi is nectar, but it has been laced with the poison of wrong understanding. So, do I say, 'No, I won't eat it'? I'm hungry. I want food. I need the nectar to take care of this body." She said, "Like that, over a period of time, I have gotten rid of the poison in my life and I have kept the nectar."

What I want to share with all of you is this: Don't throw the good things away. See the nectar. Take the nectar. Simply get rid of the poison.

FROM DARKNESS TO LIGHT

In the *Guru Gītā*, in verse 23, we sing, *gukāras-tvandhakāraśca rukāras-teja ucyate*. "The syllable *gu* indicates darkness and the syllable *ru* indicates light."

When you are in the darkness, you don't understand any of this because you are ignorant. But when you are in the light, when you are in the Self, when you are in Consciousness, all of this makes great sense.

Here is something you could do at home. Take a piece of paper. Draw a line down the middle. On one side, write *gu*, meaning darkness. On the other side, write *ru*, meaning light. Then look at your life and fill in the two sides.

The idea is to look at what is poison, what is darkness. Eliminate that and focus upon the light.

This same verse says, *ajñāna-grāsakaṁ brahma gurureva na saṁśayaḥ*. "There is no doubt about what the Guru, the grace-bestowing power, does in our life."

If you choose to sit in a dark room and say, "It's dark. It's cold. It's dark. It's cold," you cannot do anything. You have to come out of that room. Sit in the sun and say, "Wow! Feel the warmth of the sun."

Of course, my mother always advised me, "Avoid the sun from 11 a.m. to 4 p.m." Similarly, sometimes you have to go away, you have to hide from the Guru, because you have to digest what you are eating. Otherwise, you'll get diarrhea because you're eating too much. The knowledge you receive has to be digested.

Whenever somebody asks me, "What was the best time of your life?" I say, "Without a doubt, April 1978 to October 1982." Those were the days, months, and years I spent in the physical company of Baba Muktānanda.

But—I want to tell everyone—don't be too historical about those days. That is a mistake many of us make. The Guru is alive today. The Guru is present in your life in this very moment.

Yesterday, as we sat here chanting the *Guru Gītā* in the morning, I wrote down a few verses. I have chosen six. The version of the *Guru Gītā* we sing has 182 verses. There are many different versions because people come along and think, "I'm going to make it better. I'm going to delete some verses I think make no sense, and I'm going to add some that make good sense."

I tell them, "It's fine the way it is."

Verse 21 says,

ananyāś-cintayanto māṁ
sulabhaṁ paramaṁ padam,
tasmāt sarva-prayatnena
guror-ārādhanaṁ kuru.

Ananya is a name for girls in India. It means unbroken. Lord Śiva says to Pārvatī, "Let the mind never stop thinking of the Guru. Let it just focus on the Guru."

And then, *sulabham paramam padam*. He says, "That attainment is so easy." How so? He says, "Constantly, with effort, without being lazy, follow what the Guru has said."

Somebody might say *ārādhanam* means to worship the Guru. But worshipping the Guru doesn't mean that you go to the Guru and say, "Guruji, I'll squeeze your legs."

The Guru would say, "Excuse me, it's hurting." That happens, you know.

The person says, "But that's what it says here in the *Guru Gītā*."

The Guru says, "I think it means that you should live the teachings."

The relationship between Guru and disciple is the fruit of many lifetimes. I've shared before that wherever I find myself today is not an accident. It's something that has come about over lifetimes.

Where you are is not just because of what you've done, it's also because of all those along with you. Somebody in your family whom you don't even know may be praying for you, doing something for you, or thinking about you. They may not know why, but they are.

There is a devotee in Ahmedabad who has often shared a

story with us. He and his father and mother and sisters used to come to Ganeshpuri in an Ambassador car. One morning, Baba came out at 4 o'clock, just as they were leaving. They had to drive eight hours to get back home. They had already told Baba the night before that they were going and said their goodbyes. But Baba came out in the morning and asked the guard, "Which is the car that is going to Ahmedabad?"

The guard pointed to the car, and Baba took his stick and went around to all four tires and hit them.

The devotee said, "We don't understand what the Guru did. Maybe we were going to have a flat. Maybe the car was going to have a problem. All we know is that the guard told us this. We never asked Baba why he did what he did."

Verse 73 says,

aneka-janma-samprāpta-
sarva-karma-vidāhine,
svātmajñāna-prabhāveṇa
tasmai śrīgurave namaḥ.

The collection of good karmas from so many lifetimes finally gives you *svātmajñāna*—the knowledge of the Self. And then you offer salutations to Śrī Guru for this.

Verse 87 says,

dhyānaṁ śṛṇu mahādevi
sarvānanda-pradāyakam,
sarva-saukhyakaraṁ nityaṁ
bhukti-mukti-vidhāyakam.

Lord Śiva says to Pārvatī, "Listen carefully because the Guru gives you love-bliss."

So, when you think of the Guru, think of light. Think of the khichdi. In the West it is known as comfort food.

Sarva-saukhyakaraṁ nityam. I want you to understand this word, *saukhya*. Those of you who own dogs will understand it.

When its boss or owner returns home—it doesn't matter who it is: man, woman, whatever—the dog becomes tranquil, content. Everything's okay. *Saukhya*. Even if one member of the family is missing, the dog sits at the door until that person comes back.

Nityam means always, eternal, without fail. It describes the bond, the relationship, the friendship, the attachment, the love. Happiness to many people means "I'm happy when I get my ice cream. I'm happy when I get my Pepto-Bismol after lunch." Their happiness depends upon all these factors.

The scriptures tell us that when we do our practice, when we do our sādhanā, then both *bhukti* and *mukti*, both the pleasures of the world and the liberation of the Self, will come to us.

You may wonder, "What should I worship the Guru for? Why should I worship God? Why should I be spiritual?" The only thing I would say is that life in this world is nothing without prayer. The level of prayer doesn't matter. Prayer itself is what's important—your connection to divinity, to Truth. That brings you *sarva-saukhya*.

Verse 169 says,

mātā dhanyā pitā dhanyo
dhanyo vaṁśaḥ kulaṁ tathā,
dhanyā ca vasudhā devi
guru-bhaktiḥ sudurlabhā.

It says, "The mother is blessed, and the father is blessed. The entire clan is blessed." Nor is it just the family and the ancestors; *vasudhā* means this earth. The earth, too, feels blessed by God, by the Guru.

And the verse says *guru-bhaktiḥ sudurlabhā*. This love we feel for the Guru—this emotion, this longing, this absorption, this affection—is rare indeed. Here in the ashram, you might think, "Oh, so many of us feel this." But go to Times Square. You will realize how many don't feel this. The contrast is huge between those who believe, who trust, and those who don't.

Why? Verse 90 says,

nityaṁ śuddhaṁ nirābhāsaṁ
nirākāraṁ nirañjanam,
nityabodhaṁ cidānandaṁ
guruṁ brahma namāmyaham.

These are the qualities of the Self—the qualities of divinity, of Truth—that dwell within each and every one us.

One quality of the Self is nityam. It's eternal; it's always there. Whether you believe in it or you don't believe in it, the Self is always there. Nothing can happen to it.

It's *śuddham*. It's pure. It's *nirañjanam*. It's untainted. It's *nirākāram*. It cannot be touched. It's *nirābhāsam*. You can't even actually feel it.

When we were in California, one of the transcribers of Baba's talks said, "I've had *śaktipāt*. I've experienced it. I know it. But still I don't know what it is."

That's why this verse says nirābhāsam: you can't know the Self the way you know, say, ice cream. You can take a slurp of ice cream, right? You can't do that with śaktipāt or with the Self. You just sense what is happening inside you. You know you have been touched.

The way I would describe it is to say that the Self, Consciousness, the Truth we seek is always in the light. We might sometimes retreat into darkness. We can sometimes get lost in our ignorance. But the Self, the Truth, is always in light. Why? It is *nityabodham*. It is self-illuminating; it's constantly illumined. It's constantly in light.

Within yourself, when you are in that space of light, of Truth, all that you can know is knowledge. All that you can know is wisdom. That wisdom is *cidānandam*. It is the bliss of Consciousness.

Therefore, *guruṁ brahma namāmyaham*. I offer salutations to the Guru.

When somebody grabs you and says, "There's only darkness, there's only poison," you say, "No, no, no. There's only light.

There's only light. There's only light." Got it?

This is why, whenever struggles come, you have to be clear within yourself about what the Guru has given. Don't get lost. Don't look at the poison. Look at the khichdi. Look at the light. Look at the Truth.

YOU ARE BLESSED

With great respect and love, I would like to welcome you all to our Intensive here this morning. Take a moment to quiet your mind, to make yourself even more still.

Our topic this morning is Śiva *dṛṣṭi*, the vision of Śiva.

We want our mind to have the awareness of that vision, to be able to see the Absolute. We want that as we hear these teachings, we're able to understand and bring ourselves to that vision. So slow down your mind. Allow your thoughts to quieten. Bring yourself to absolute stillness. The only way you will understand is if you allow yourself to sit here with expanded awareness. Put logic aside. Don't try to reason with what you hear this morning. Simply go into your heart and try to see how you can bring this awareness into your life.

I'll begin with the story of a saint. In the Indian tradition, we have a celestial sage named Nārada. As he is traveling around the Earth, he spends a night with a couple. The couple have no children, so they ask him to bless them with a child.

Nārada goes to the Lord and puts forth their request.

The Lord looks at their karma and tells Nārada that it is not possible for them to have children in this lifetime.

Nārada returns to the Earth and tells the couple, "The Lord says in this lifetime, due to your karma, it is not possible for you to have children."

The couple accept this and go about their life.

One day a saint comes to their house and spends the night with them. The next morning, as he is leaving, he blesses them. That blessing bears fruit, and they have children.

Some years later, Nārada visits them again, and he sees the children in the house. He asks the couple, "Whose children are these?"

The man says, "They are ours."

Nārada asks, "How did that come about?"

The man says, "A saint visited us, and he blessed us. This is the fruit of his blessing."

Nārada is rather upset. He goes back to the Lord and says, "When I asked you to grant that couple children, you told me it was not in their karma to have children. But now they have children!"

The Lord laughs and says, "That must be the work of a saint."

Baba Muktānanda would tell us that the mind cannot understand the touch of a saint, the magic a saint performs in each of our lives.

Just as the couple were blessed with children, each one of us is blessed in our own way. All we need to do is be open and allow our mind and our heart to receive the grace and the blessings that come our way.

Ultimately, words themselves are not so important. The original scriptural texts from India were written in Sanskrit. Very few people today know Sanskrit. Baba wrote down his thought process in Hindi, and that Hindi was translated into English. Today I am speaking to you in English, telling you how I understand the teachings. You will hear the translation in Spanish, according to the translator's understanding. She is Mexican, and you will hear her words in your Argentinian way. We have Sanskrit, we have Hindi, we have English, we have me, we have the translator, and we have you. So we have six levels of language before the teachings can even penetrate!

THE OUTLOOK OF ŚIVA

The teaching of Śiva dṛṣṭi, the outlook of Śiva, comes from the philosophy of Kashmir Shaivism. In *Secret of the Siddhas*, Baba talks about how we can have this outlook.

In this world, we experience two kinds of objects: that which is sentient, and that which is insentient. To put it another way, there is matter, and then there are conscious beings. In all of this, we want to experience Śiva. To regard all that happens as the embodiment of Śiva is to have the outlook of Śiva.

At different times, different beings have shared with us this outlook. They have tried to express to us that the Absolute is everywhere. Baba Muktānanda says we have to wear the glasses of that outlook, and then we can see things in that way. The mind has to come to the experience of the Absolute.

However, our mindset, our experience, is limited by time, by space, by circumstances. Before we can understand that the universe is the embodiment of Śiva, we must first understand these limitations.

We are bound by time. By time, I mean whatever has happened in our life in the past, whatever is happening now in the present, and whatever we imagine might or can or should or could happen in the future.

We are bound by space. In our own mind, we can only see what is in the space around us. We aren't aware of what is happening outside this room.

And we are bound circumstances. We believe that all circumstances are created by me.

In the experience of Śiva, of the Absolute—which is perfect, which is complete, which is omnipotent—these limitations do not exist. Śiva is extremely independent, not bound by time, space, and circumstances. Śiva is the embodiment of Consciousness.

Śiva has created this world through his *icchā-śakti*, which is his will, and his *kriyā-śakti*, which is his action.

Now, each one of us also has our own icchā-śakti, which is our individual will. And each one of us has kriya-śakti, which is our power of action. But we use our icchā and our kriyā in limited ways. We live our lives the way we do, but the sage is asking us to expand our awareness.

In the scriptures, there is a story. In it, there is a meeting of all the celestial beings, and the Lord of Death also arrives at this meeting. As he walks in, he sees a bird up in a tree.

The King of Birds sees the Lord of Death looking at that bird. The King of Birds thinks, "I should protect this bird from the Lord of Death." So he sends the bird far away.

Of course, the bird dies when it reaches that place.

The King of Birds asks the Lord of Death, "Why did you look at that bird?"

The Lord of Death says, "Well, my records showed that that bird had to be at that particular place. When I saw it here, I wondered how its death would take place there, when it was here. But thanks to you, he was diverted to the right place for his death."

A sage is not limited by time and space. But our mind is limited by these things. So we want to ask ourselves, "How can I become free of these things?" Intellectually, you may understand a teaching. But that's not enough. In the midst of the experience of life, you have to think about how you can achieve it.

I AM THAT

The philosophy of Shaivism says we have to remind ourselves that Śiva pervades equally in all forms, and is formless as well. When the understanding develops within us that the universe is not different from Śiva, we begin to see Śiva everywhere.

The sages tell us to contemplate, "I am the Absolute."

As we sit today to meditate, as we breathe in and out, the mind can become aware of the mantra *Haṁsa*. As we breathe in, we breathe in the awareness "I am." As we breathe out, we breathe out the awareness "That."

As much as you think you have to remind yourself, "I am That," ultimately you simply have to sit in the awareness of *Haṁsa*, "I am That." "That" is your real nature, and because it is your real nature, you simply have to become aware of it. You don't have to tell yourself, "I am That. I am That. I am That."

The awareness you have developed—"I am a man." "I am a woman." "I am a boy." "I am a girl."—is just one or another identification related to the external body. When you go beyond this physical body, you come to the realization, "I am Śiva" or "I am Śakti."

The sages tell us Śiva and Śakti are not different from each other. In truth, Śiva and Shakti are one. Through Śakti, Śiva controls the activities of this universe.

Right now, you think, "I'm thinking." You think, "I'm going to do." You think, "I understand." However, when you come to the awareness of Śiva, of the Absolute, and sit in that awareness, then you see that your will is really Śiva's will, your action is really Śiva's action, your knowledge is really Śiva's knowledge. With the outlook of Śiva, you see that your icchā and kriya and *jñāna* (knowledge) all belong to Śiva.

The sages tell us to offer everything to the Absolute at all times. They tell us not to think, "I am the doer."

When we get caught in the thought process of "I need to be acknowledged for what I do," our struggle in life becomes all about recognition. The sages say that idiots only talk about what they will do. They say egoistical people boast about what they have done. But a sage simply does whatever he does, and doesn't say anything about it.

You can ask yourself: which of these three categories do I fall into? Do I only talk about what I will do? Do I boast about what I have done? Or do I simply do what needs to be done, and not worry about it?

In your humility, you have to come to the experience of Śiva. When you allow devotion to be awakened within you, you begin to recognize Śiva everywhere.

A NATURAL PRACTICE

There is a story about St. Augustine. He tries for a long time to understand divinity. He studies a lot and he searches a lot, but he finds nothing.

One night, he has a dream. In the dream, he is walking along the seashore, and he sees a small child sitting near the water. The child has a small cup, and he seems troubled.

Augustine goes close to the child and asks, "What's the matter?"

The child explains that he is trying to scoop up the ocean inside his cup.

Augustine laughs and says, "My child, the ocean will never fit inside a cup!"

The child looks at Augustine and says, "How is what I'm trying to do different from what you're trying to do? You want to scoop God into your little cup."

As Augustine is thinking about this, the child says, "Let me show you how it can be done." And the child throws the cup into the ocean.

Augustine immediately got it. He saw that he had to allow himself to merge into the Absolute.

Each of us has to understand this teaching of the Absolute in this manner. Bound by time, bound by space, bound by circumstance, we cannot understand that great outlook. We cannot understand that expanded awareness. We have to let go of all of these limitations.

They say a child recognizes its parents, and it is natural for a child to do so. In the same way, through scriptural truth, the Guru brings us to the recognition of the Absolute.

In truth, there is nothing we have to do except bring ourselves to the understanding that the means of attainment, the goal that is attained, the attainment, the one who attains, the one who enjoys, that which is enjoyed—all is the Absolute.

Think for a moment, "Who is meditating? What am I meditating upon? Who is performing the act of meditation?" When you slowly dissolve all of these differences or dualities, you come to the understanding that all of it is Śiva.

The *Yoga Vāsiṣṭha* says, "The world is as you see it." What is this world? According to this teaching, this entire world is Śiva.

Hopefully by the end of the day today at least some portion of your mind will come to this experience.

I find that because they don't understand this teaching, some seekers make a joke out of it; they make fun of it. When the mind makes it a joke, this outlook doesn't become a natural practice.

Let's try to understand and actually experience this outlook of Śiva. Yes, it happens over time. Yet we have to constantly remind ourselves. The more we remind ourselves, the more frequent that experience becomes.

Shaivism says we have to have firm conviction. The mind cannot doubt. The mind cannot wander. And as I said just now, we can't take the teaching lightly. If you want to attain this outlook, that will only happen if you make it your natural state.

The Guru's touch, the Guru's word, the Guru's mantra, and the sādhanā given by the Guru all lead to this outlook. The *Upaniṣads* tell us to practice sādhanā with the following awareness: "I am a form of Śiva. I will attain Śiva. By becoming him, I will attain him. And because I am Śiva, I will attain Śivahood very easily."

Now, you have to think of the young boy who throws the cup into the ocean. Each of us is the cup, is the body. Instead of trying to find Śiva in your limited sense, allow yourself to throw this limitation into the ocean, which is Śiva.

The *Upaniṣad* continues, "Although I appear to be different, I am one with Śiva. The entire universe is the activity of Śiva. Śiva experiences everything. It is essential to know Śiva. Being Śiva, I will attain Śiva. Śiva is the experiencer and what is being experienced. While remaining Śiva, I will attain Śiva. Śiva is the doer, Śiva is the action. Even though I am involved with all my senses, I am Śiva."

In this way, we become established in the awareness of Śiva. A mature seeker, through constantly reminding himself or herself, becomes one with Śiva. This is the essence of Śiva dṛṣṭi.

Our mind flutters like a butterfly. In contrast, the steadiness of a siddha, who has the vision of oneness, reminds us of the possibility of stillness. That stillness can erupt within you, and suddenly you are stunned by the shift in your own mind. For a moment, you experience freedom.

When you receive śaktipāt from the Guru, it propels you into the stillness of your own mind, where you are enthralled by Consciousness itself. This is the gift a siddha gives us, which the siddha has received from his or her own Guru. The disciple who receives this gift discovers that he or she is equally conscious, equally as great as the Guru.

What an ignorant person creates is different from what another ignorant person creates, because each individual's creation depends on his or her understanding. But once we come to know the Truth, the entire world appears as the embodiment of Śiva.

We simply have to allow ourselves to give way and allow grace to bring us to the outlook of Śiva. Then, when we come to that state, there is no subject, there is no object. There is simply the blissful, supreme Śiva. We have the recognition that Śiva, the Absolute, manifests in all of these innumerable forms of multiplicity.

RESPONSIBILITY

With great love and respect, I'd like to welcome everyone to our satsaṅg here this morning.

We are on our second-to-the-last Sunday for the second term of this year. We were here in April, we went to Argentina, and we are here now. Then I go to India and come back in September and stay through October and November.

This week we have our youth retreat. As a kid, I used to look at people who were thirty years old and think—probably like the young ones are doing now—"Wow. That man looks old." However, as time goes on and you experience life, you begin to think, "I wish I knew then what I know now."

I will be fifty-six this October. The grey tells on me. When I was twenty and first came on the seat, when Baba Muktānanda had just left his body, everybody kept saying, "You're so young." At that time, I wished I had a long grey or white beard and looked sagely and wise. But now I think it might be nice if it were black.

This month, Shanti Mandir completes thirty-one years of existence. This ashram completes nineteen years of existence. I believe it is wonderful to be part of a tradition and a lineage that will continue long after we are gone.

The times we live in are all about change, about new things. I won't go into too many details because that topic can get controversial. I'll let you use your great imagination to figure it out. But one thing we can say about our world today is that people think in a selfish manner; they think about "me," about "I."

The teachings tell us to think about *sarve*, about all, about everyone. Whatever action we may perform, we have to realize it has an effect, an outcome.

Somebody might say, "Why should I worry about that?"

When you do something, you have to think not just about what pleases you and your life but about the effects your action will have a couple of generations down. Those generations pay for that which their ancestors have done.

The philosophy of karma tells us to ask ourselves about the

purpose of our actions. Satsaṅg inspires us to ask, "What is it that I want to do? And what is it that is meant to be done?"

New things are exciting. I don't deny that. But then, later on, what happens to that newness? What is the outcome of that newness?

If you have read the news in the past month or two, and even before that, there's been a lot of talk about fish eating plastic and animals eating plastic. I recently saw a picture of a fawn, a baby deer, with a plastic bag in its mouth. In India, many people throw away food in a plastic bag, and a cow may pick up that plastic bag to eat the food. There are reports that when a cow was operated upon, so many kilograms of plastic were found inside the stomach of that cow. A cow, as most of you know, has four stomachs. The food is eaten, it sits, it is brought up, the cow chews it, and then the food goes back down and is digested in the system. So digestion has four levels. The human also has a very intricate and complex system of digestion.

So, we perform an action, and that action has an effect. The first word that comes to mind is *responsibility*.

Most of the year, we're like a family living here. Sometimes I hear through the grapevine that the little fridge has food rotting in it. If you're living alone, you could say, "Yes, that's my food." But if we are a family of twenty, say, you would have to ask, "Are the other nineteen blind, that they don't see the food rotting?" Some people write their names on their food items. So if rotting food is claimed by one person, the nineteen blind people can tell the person who owns the food that it is rotting.

I'll share a story. King Akbar is ruling Delhi and the surrounding area and he asks his prime minister, Birbal, "How many blind people are in our area?"

Birbal says, "Give me some days and I will give you a count."

Birbal takes an attendant with him and goes to the middle of the marketplace. He sits there sewing. When people see the prime minister in the middle of Delhi, sewing, they come up and ask, "Birbal, are you sewing?"

When each comes up, Birbal tells his attendant, "Write his name down."

News about this travels to the king, and he comes the marketplace to check out what's happening. He says, "Birbal, are you sewing here in the marketplace?"

Birbal doesn't answer the question, he just says, "Write his name down."

The next day Birbal goes to court and says to the king, "I'll come to court tomorrow and give you the answer."

The next day everybody gathers because they're curious: what has Birbal been doing in the marketplace sewing?

Birbal arrives in court the next day and says, "O Your Majesty, this is the list of the blind people, and you are one of them."

The other day, a bunch of ashramites were putting beds together in Mukteshwari, and somebody came by and asked, "What is it that you are putting together?"

One person said, "Isn't it obvious? We are putting beds together. You can see one that's already been put together."

So, if that is my food rotting in the fridge, am I blind or am I purposely allowing others to be tortured by my rotting food? That's the kind of question we can ask in satsaṅg. We sit here, we listen.

People say to me, "Tell people to think,"

I say, "What do you think I do every Sunday?"

Then people say, "I don't agree with you."

It's not that they agree with me or don't agree with me, it's just that it's too much work for them to think. It's too much work to be responsible.

Being responsible means that I am answerable for the actions performed by me.

COOPERATION

My second word is *cooperation.* In India, we have a lot of cooperatives. We have cooperative farms and cooperative banks. Not corporations. I want to clarify the difference: there is a corporation—which is a business that is incorporated—and there is cooperation. The word cooperation has two parts: co and operation.

We'll see a lot of cooperation here this week with the young people. They'll make friends with each other and they'll get along. We are supposed to do that as humans. We are supposed to be responsible. We are supposed to cooperate.

I remember a joke from back in the 1980s, when I was traveling. An Indian goes to the U.K. for the first time. An Englishman says, "Sir, would you like a cup of tea?"

The Indian says no.

So the Englishman doesn't do anything.

About twenty minutes into their conversation, the Indian says, "Where's my cup of tea?"

The Englishman says, "You said no."

The Indian says, "Well, we say that. But your job is to serve it anyway."

This tradition continues even today in different parts of the world. It's considered humble to say, "No, no. Me? No, no chai. I would really like one, but no."

In this tradition, in all the countries where this "no" habit exists, you are forced to show people your love.

People say offering food is an expression of love. I don't deny that, but you also have to consider the other person, right? For example, when you are offering somebody food, maybe he's already had his fill.

I tell people, "If you make ten dishes, put it out like a potluck. People can choose what they want. Don't force people to take more than they want."

I have a little story about that too.

After getting married, a son-in-law is invited to his in-laws' home for a meal. It's the tradition. When the food is served, the first thing the son-in-law eats is the eggplant, aubergine, brinjal. Then he eats all the rest of his food.

The second time he visits the in-laws, eggplant is served again. Again, that's the first thing he eats.

The third time he comes, the fourth time he comes—every time eggplant is served.

The fifth time, he asks his mother-in-law, "Why is it that every time I come, you make eggplant?"

She says, "Son, I saw that it's the first thing you eat, so I figured that must be what you love most."

He says, "Let me tell you the truth. It's the one vegetable I don't like. I get rid of it on my plate so I can eat the things that I like."

She says, "You should have told me that the first time."

He says, "Well, I'm just getting comfortable enough now to be able to tell you this."

So, responsibility and cooperation need to be understood, to be figured out. Not everything is always said through the mouth. Not always does everything have to be expressed. It can be understood. I'm sure all of us sitting in this room are wise. I'm sure that we are not so blind that we can't see, that we can't understand.

I've pondered for the last few years how it is in this society that when people aren't affected directly by something, they say, "Why should I bother?"

The sages prayed, "May *all* beings be content." They could have said, "May I be content."

When they said, "May all be free of sickness," they could have said, "May I be free of sickness." When they said, "May all see auspicious sights," they could have said, "May I see auspicious sights."

"May there be no suffering for anyone" could have been "May I never, ever, ever, ever suffer."

"May I" is not the teaching. When you perform an action, don't just think about yourself. Think big.

ADAPTABILITY

The third word is *adaptability*.

When we walked in, someone said, "The radio advised, 'Go where there is air conditioning.'" Because it's going to be hot. So he said, "We'll go to Shanti Mandir."

In case you didn't notice, we don't have air conditioning. We have open doors, open windows. We have fans, mobile fans. The fan can go with us wherever we go. If we go to the living room, it can go with us. If we go to the kitchen, it can go with us. If we go to the gift shop, it could go there too.

As kids, we grew up with fans. Now everybody says, "Put the air conditioning on." It's easy. But if you read the news, you might have read recently that every air conditioner that gets turned on adds to the heat. It produces heat and pollutants outside the building.

Of course, we're lucky here that we don't have buildings right next to us. We can open up and let air flow in. But in cities such as Manhattan and Queens, and wherever else the buildings are right next to each other, the buildings create wind tunnels. The greed of real estate developers is such that they don't think about what will happen to the neighbors when they put up a new building.

This goes back to the first word, *responsibility*. It goes back to the second word, *cooperation*. And it shows us we need to learn to adapt.

In India, villages are slowly dying out. In the U.S., we still have the village of Walden. The word *village* is still used. I think villages will become more important in this world; they will become the way of the future. When I say "a village," I'm thinking of an ashram, a community like what we have here. That concept can be developed so that families live together. They have a place of worship. They have a school. The community can give a wholesome experience for each individual.

There are many details that need to be worked out, but I think this will be a necessity for human beings within the next twenty to thirty years. Real estate developers will have to rethink how they are developing household tracts, because the most important ingredient missing in our modern-day life is affection. Not love, affection.

Baba Muktānanda, in his time, created what he created. We are here today, continuing on this tradition, continuing on these practices. And we have all these young people who are getting ready, who are thinking and wondering how we move on.

The sacred tradition, the teachings, and the practices have to be maintained. We cannot throw a new spin on them. They have to remain true to what was, what is, and what will be. We aren't looking to adapt the teachings; there has to be consistency.

It is July 1 today. We've completed one half of this year 2018, which means we have completed seventeen and a half years of this twenty-first century.

"Where is the world going? Where is society going?" are questions asked by many. We don't know. It's going somewhere, that's for sure. Is it good or bad? I don't know.

I tell people again and again and again that the one quality the world is missing is affection.

They look at me as if they're wondering, "What do you mean?"

For those of you who want to understand what this means in spiritual terminology, I suggest you look up the twelfth chapter of the *Bhagavad Gītā*. It talks about devotion.

One of the words used by Lord Kṛṣṇa there is *homeless*.

In his commentary, Swami Chinmayānanda explains this by saying, "Spending a night on the railway platform or in an airport does not make it home. What makes it home is how you feel within."

A sage who has understood that his connection is really to the Divine, to the Truth, to Consciousness doesn't need any physical space to call home, to feel whole. To him, all places are home. Wherever he goes, whomsoever he is with is home.

Of course, this makes me think of Bhagavān Nityānanda, who spent most of his life free, not owning any place, not creating any place—except for the one ashram he created in South

India. Then he left that ashram also, after he realized all of a sudden, "What have I done?"

Somebody must have told him, "Create a place." So he created a place. And then he thought, "Oh my God, I'm bound." So he left it and continued on in his freedom. When he came to Ganeshpuri and lived there for the last thirty years of his life, he lived freely. As soon as any place he was staying became controlling or limiting, he just moved to another place. Finally he moved to the place where he left his body.

Freedom comes over time. It's not easy. It's easy to say, "I'm going to be free." You simply move something from the dining room to the living room or from the TV room to the den. And you say, "I'm becoming free of it." You're not really becoming free of it. You're just manipulating it.

One word for contentment in Sanskrit is *sukha*. So, let us become sukha, content. Let us become comfortable within ourselves, or as you say in English, comfortable in our own skin.

You have to feel good. You have to feel complete. You have to feel whole. Only then can you share your goodness, your affection.

Thank you all for being here this morning.

THE RIVER DOESN'T DRINK ITS OWN WATER

It is with great respect and love that I would like to welcome everyone here this morning. Namaste!

The scriptures talk to us about learning, and about contemplating and imbibing what we learn. First we learn by hearing or by reading. But the other two are even more important: contemplating and imbibing.

For example, if you jump in a lake, you will get wet. But if you wear a wetsuit—like you do when you go into the cold ocean—then you won't get wet. Often when we come to the Guru as seekers, it's like we have a wetsuit in our mind. We don't imbibe the teachings. We see the waves. We ride the waves. That's easy enough. But the quality of imbibing—of actually getting wet—is the most difficult, I think.

That is because there's already a "me," there's already an "I." And that me, that I, is like a wetsuit that keeps us dry.

At every Intensive with Baba Muktānanda, one of the swamis would wave a coconut in the hall and then go out and break it. Often the first speaker would say, "You saw the coconut being waved. The idea is to break the coconut because its hard shell represents the ego. Within that shell is the sweet water, the delicious fruit of the coconut, the inner Self."

Because of all that has happened in our lives, we feel vulnerable when we break open the coconut, the ego. At different times, we may have opened ourselves, but society being what it is, we then closed up again.

As you listen, contemplate, and imbibe, this begins to make sense. You come to a place within where, whether you're being praised or you're being criticized, you are not affected by either. I know it's not easy to do. But slowly, the flame within rises more and more and more. And then you go out into this world as light.

There is a Sanskrit verse that says, "The river never drinks its own water. The trees don't eat their own fruit. The clouds water the crop but never eat that crop. Good people are always thinking about upliftment."

We always hear the last part: benefit others, act for the

upliftment of others. A great person always thinks, “What can I do that will uplift?”

GIVE WHAT
YOU WANT TO GET

As we think about upliftment, we can also think about karma yoga. Karma yoga is the yoga of action.

In the modern-day world, we are told to act, to be a doer. But the sages always tell us to act with a purpose. Activity, action, should always have a goal.

Recently, somebody asked me, "Do you think I should always have a purpose?"

I said, "If you have no purpose, you'll be like a hamster. Your actions will have no output, no fruits, or no results."

In the *Bhagavad Gītā*, Kṛṣṇa is trying to convince Arjuna that doing is important. Arjuna asks, "Should I do or should I not do?" Kṛṣṇa tells him, "Arjuna, it is your duty to perform the action."

If you have a human body, if you have a life, then perform actions.

But don't think about what you will get if you perform that action. That's how we mostly do things. We think, "If I have worked eight hours, I need to be paid for eight hours. I have given you this much, so I should get this much back."

When parents raise a child, they are always saying, "Look at all we have sacrificed to raise you! Therefore, we expect you to give us back that which we have given."

And the child says, "I never asked you to bring me onto this earth. I never told you I wanted a human form. It was you, out of your own desire, who created me. And then, as good parents, you took care of me and raised me. You did what was your duty."

An example that is used in the scriptures is the sandalwood tree. Sandalwood is cooling. I put sandalwood paste on my forehead, and we also put it on these statues. I especially like the quality and fragrance of sandalwood that is grown in the southern part of India.

It is said, "A sandalwood tree does not grow for its own comfort. It gives comfort to others when it is applied to the body. It is the same with noble people. They live for the purpose of giving."

In our society, we always think, “What will I get? How will I benefit?” Yet today I am only talking about the opposite: “How I can give?”

In the *Kaṭha Upaniṣad*, Nāciketa’s father has a fire ceremony. In those days, the tradition was to give a cow to each brahmin. India was an agricultural country, so everybody had bulls, cows, and so on.

Nāciketa’s father thinks, “I’ll give all my old cows.” In other words, those cows that can’t have babies, that can’t give milk.

Young Nāciketa is upset. He wants his father to give away possessions with some value so his sacrifice will be meaningful. So he says, “I also belong to you. To whom will you give me?” He asks this two or three times.

His father gets angry and says, “I give you to the Lord of Death!”

The whole *Upaniṣad* is based on the conversation that takes place between Nāciketa and the Lord of Death. Nāciketa is upset because he thought he had a good father.

We see the same situation in India today. When you go to a shop and say, “I want these things, the shopkeeper asks, “Is this for a pūjā?”

You say, “Yes.”

He says, “Okay, I’ll give you this old box.” The old box contains all the cheap stuff that doesn’t sell in his shop.

I always tell people, “When you want to give, think of what you want to get.”

A sādhu comes to town. A woman wants her son to have children. It is a tradition that when you come to a holy man, you never come empty handed. You come with something. And then you receive his blessings, and you take home the fruit of that blessing.

So the woman brings the sādhu some bananas. As she was buying the bananas, the shopkeeper said, “This bunch is so many rupees, and this other bunch is so many rupees. And the really ripe ones are the cheapest.” So she bought those.

She puts them in front of the sādhu. He blesses her. And she goes home.

A couple of years later, she has grandkids. They are a little disabled. So she waits for the sādhu to come back to town, which he does.

When she sees him, she says, " I came to you with bananas and I asked for blessings. I was blessed. But the children are a little disabled."

The sādhu says, "And how were the bananas?"

So we come to a holy being, we pray, but we always think, "Really, it's just a token that I am giving. I am not really giving."

RIPEN AS YOU AGE

The scripture says, "The sun sets every day, taking away part of our lifespan." Every day the sun sets, it's one less twelve-hour day. In the summer, it's a little bit more. Winters are a little bit less. But in the Indian tradition, we believe it's a twelve-hour day, from sunrise to sunset.

Some part of your life is gone when the sun has set. So you should contemplate every day, "What good deeds have I done today?"

In the ancient culture, all that was to be done was done from sunrise to sunset. From sunrise to sunset, there was light, there was daytime. That was the time to give and take. And once the sun set, boom! No more business to be conducted. Everybody went home. Everybody stayed inside because it was dark outside. That was the time to pray, meditate, chant, be with family, eat, sleep.

I tell people that our elders teach us many things, if we want to learn. Good elders, that is. Because we have bad elders too. The good elders teach us good things.

We all will be elders someday. All of us should slowly ripen as we age. When a fruit is ripe, three things can happen to it. First, when you see most fruit ripen, its color changes. Second, it becomes soft as it ripens. And finally, it becomes sweet, it becomes delicious.

As each individual matures, or ripens, there may not be a visible change of color in his or her skin. But the person's nature, or way of being, changes. The person becomes gentler.

The Gujarati poet-saint Narsinh Mehta wrote a poem that Mahatma Gandhi used to sing a lot. In it, he says, "He is called a person of God who understands the pain and the suffering of others. There is no trace of ego when he wants to help someone."

Here's a story I read. One day it is raining, and a teacher is inside teaching his class. He asks his students, "If I were to give you a hundred rupees, what would you do with it?"

Different children answer different things. Today, if students were asked that question, one would say, "I will buy a video game." Another would say, "I'll buy Nintendo." Or "I'll buy a baseball bat." Or "I'll buy a cricket bat." Or "I'll buy chocolate."

One child, however, is lost in thought.

The teacher says to him, "What are you thinking?"

He says, "I think I'll buy my mother a pair of glasses."

The teacher says, "Why do you want to do that?"

He says, "I don't have a father. My mother is the one who takes care of the family, and she sews for a living. That's how I can come to school. So if I buy her glasses, she'll be able to see better. She'll stitch better, and she'll have more sales. We'll all live more comfortably."

The teacher goes up to him, gives him the hundred rupees, and says, "This is a loan. Whenever in life you have the ability to do so, come back and return this hundred rupees."

Almost twenty years go by in the story. Again, it's raining—I think the storyteller likes rain. In India, we have districts, like you have towns here. The highest person in a district in India is the district collector. He's in charge of many legal things. So at this school, on this rainy day, along comes the district collector's car, with its red light.

Everybody in the school is a little worried when they see the car. They wonder whether they have done something wrong that caused the officer to come to their school.

The car stops. The collector gets out and goes up to the teacher, who is now twenty years older. He says, "I'm the boy to whom you gave a hundred rupees twenty years ago. You told me to come back when I was able to return it."

The teacher is very happy. He picks up the collector, who's bowing at his feet, and hugs him.

The storyteller tells us, "Become famous but not arrogant. Be simple but don't be weak." Life changes very quickly. Even an emperor sometimes becomes a beggar. And sometimes a beggar becomes an emperor.

THREE QUALITIES OF GIVING

In the seventeenth chapter of the *Bhagavad Gītā*, Kṛṣṇa talks about *sāttva*, *rajas*, and *tamas*, the three different qualities. Kṛṣṇa says giving has the qualities of sāttva, rajas, and tamas.

We think, "I am just giving." Even the act of giving falls under these three qualities.

Kṛṣṇa says, "That which is given, knowing it to be a duty, at the proper time and place, to a worthy person from whom we expect nothing, is considered *sāttvika*."

Many organizations have the names of their donors on the buildings. At Shanti Mandir, we've always prayed that blessings will come, goodness will come, without a name plate. When we built Namaste, some of the windows were on the expensive side. Somebody said, "I'll donate, but I need a name plate on the window." I didn't think that would quite fit. Fortunately, God was kind, and somebody else came along and donated the windows, without asking for a name plate.

This is what Kṛṣṇa is talking about here: "That which is given to the right person, at the right time, in the right place, without any expectation of return." That's sāttvika giving, pure giving.

When you really think about it, that's how it works in life. Nothing is really ours to keep, because it was never ours to begin with. It's only there for as long as it is, and then it moves on.

The scriptures tell us pain and suffering arise only when we have attachment.

A tree gives its fruits. It does not make any distinction between who will enjoy the fruits and who will not. Somebody may even cut down the tree from which he has eaten the fruit. But still the tree gives its fruit. We can also give like that.

The *rājasika* type, Kṛṣṇa says, is "a gift that is given with the view to receiving something in return or given while looking for the fruit or given reluctantly."

Many of our gifts given during the course of everyday, worldly activity fall under this category. In the United States, people celebrate Black Friday. Here, we had Pink Friday yesterday. Somebody gives us a gift. And now we feel obligated to return one that is 125 percent of the original gift. You received a pillow this big, so you think, "I can't give back a pillow of the same size. I have to give one that's a bit bigger." Which then creates a dilemma for the other person. Next Christmas, he has to figure out how big a pillow to give in return.

The last one is the *tāmasika* type, Kṛṣṇa says it is "a gift given in the wrong place, at the wrong time, by an unworthy person, without respect, with insult."

It's like, "Here, take it!" We do that sometimes when we're angry or upset.

A man is told by an astrologer that he must donate a gold coin, and that gold coin will solve his problem. But the gold coin can only be given to a priest who does trikāla sandhyā. In India, priests pray in the morning at sunrise, pray at noon, and pray at night. It's their personal prayer and it's called *trikāla sandhyā*.

To find a priest today who does even one prayer is difficult. Finally, this man finds one elderly priest. So he goes to him and gives him the gold coin.

The priest gives his blessing to the man from whom he takes the gold coin. He does this by making a prayer, an intention, as he pours water over the coin. It is said that when he lets go of the water, the skin on his hand that touched the gold coin is burned.

He has given the *puṇya*, the merit, of his sandhyā, to that man. In exchange for what he has given, he has taken on the man's karma through that gold coin.

What we're talking about is subtle shifts, subtle movements, subtle energy, that cannot be seen through the physical eyes, that cannot be heard through the physical ears. When traditional Indian priests give you prasād, they give it to you like this. There is no touching. When you become sensitive, you start to feel that static electricity. Otherwise, you feel nothing.

Today, we share straws, we share spoons, we share forks, we share food from plates, without thinking. We think, "It's just food." But when you're taking something from someone else, there is a shift, a movement of energy.

How much of sāttva, how much of rajas, and how much of tamas is there inside your physical body is something you need to think about. Nobody else can do it for you. There is no thermometer you can buy, unfortunately, to tell you. I wish there was. Then you could just put it in your mouth and say, "Okay, I'm sāttvika." Or "I'm rājasika." Or "I'm tāmasika."

Maybe when we started, you thought you were only going to hear that "the river doesn't drink its own water, and the tree doesn't eat its own fruit." But how does the tree not eat its own fruit? How does the river not drink its own water? What does that mean for us?

The answer is in the activity, the effort we put forth. We all put forth effort. The tree is putting forth the effort of creating the fruit. The river is still running. Our effort to give cannot make us bound. It cannot bind us. Our effort has to free us. Our learning must lead us to liberation. The knowledge, the wisdom, we gather has to lead us to liberation. Otherwise, our activity only brings exertion.

With great respect and love, I'd like to welcome you here

BECOME STEADY

to satsaṅg this evening. It is our third evening, and what should have been the final evening. But we will have an evening tomorrow as well, with a dancing kirtan.

We began this journey a couple of weeks ago, after our final satsaṅg at the ashram in Gujarat, India. For two months, we will be on the road—first in Western Australia, now here in Eastern Australia, in Melbourne, through California, and Hawaii. We'll meet many people, including some who have been part of this tradition since before I was born, who lived with Baba Muktānanda, and who have been following this path of yoga and meditation.

As we started the tour, I was thinking about what message to carry with us. And I always feel we could do better. We could improve.

For example, when people play the *pakhawaj*, it is tuned. Yet because of the weather, sometimes it gets sharp. And sometimes it gets flat. The same is true for most instruments that need tuning. The weather affects them.

The weather affects us too. We go along. We're good. Everything's fine. And then we hit some turbulent weather.

In an airplane, all of a sudden, the pilot says, "Okay, put your seat belt on. There's some turbulence coming up. We're stopping the service. Flight attendants, please sit down." So there's no coffee, no water, nothing.

Life is like that. It's smooth. Everything's going along fine. Then all of a sudden, turbulence shows up. At that moment, we have to ask ourselves, "How am I? What is going on within myself?"

Each day we pray, "May the wicked become good. May goodness arise within each of us who lives upon this earth."

Through the process of satsaṅg, may these noble qualities arise within each and every one of us. May we feel peace. May we experience it. May we share it wherever we go.

Nobility is about thinking uplifting thoughts. It's about sharing through uplifting speech. It's about performing our activities so they are uplifting.

When we spend time in the company of one who is noble, we feel uplifted. We feel good. We benefit. Even though nothing may have transpired externally, we sense within ourselves that something wonderful has happened.

We live a noble, uplifting life not only for ourselves but also for those around us. When we do that, we begin to gather knowledge, wisdom. We begin to become wise. Then when situations arise in life, when turbulence happens, we remain steady. We don't falter. We don't lose a beat. We keep moving with that wisdom, with that understanding.

I feel that when life is turbulent, it is a test of how established we are in knowledge, in wisdom. If in that moment we forget the wisdom, the knowledge, we haven't really, as Baba Muktānanda would say, imbibed it.

Baba shared a story about a man who sells oil. He has a parrot outside his door, and he has taught this parrot to greet every customer who walks through the door by saying, "*Sītā Rām, Sītā Rām.*"

Now, there is a cat who watches this bird every single day. The owner feeds the parrot, then closes its cage, and the cat watches all that.

One day, when the owner is feeding the parrot, a customer comes in. The owner forgets to close the cage.

The cat has been waiting for this very moment. He goes and he grabs the parrot.

Baba would laugh and say, "In that moment, the parrot forgets "*Sītā Rām, Sītā Rām.*" Instead, the parrot begins making his parrot-like sounds, because now he is filled with fear. He knows death is near, waiting to finish his life.

Baba would say that, for those of us who come to satsaṅg, who follow this path, the teachings and the practices should become part of our life. Then when such situations arise, our mind doesn't waiver. Rather, our mind remains steady. It remains settled.

In Patañjali's *Yoga Sūtras*, there is a *sūtra* that says, "Not only the āsanas, the physical postures, we perform in yoga but the foundation upon which we have based our life should be steady."

Sometimes when you hold your hand out, you will see that it shakes. That shaking doesn't always come from the physical body as much as it comes from a lack of steadiness, a faltering, within. In the same way, steadiness, stillness, is what you have to find within yourself.

Where does this steadiness come from? It comes from wisdom. It comes from understanding. It comes from knowledge.

BECOME HOLY

As we move along on the path of yoga, the path of meditation, the path of satsaṅg, life actually becomes simpler. The *Upaniṣads* speak about living with a sense of detachment, a sense of renunciation. Don't become caught in the things of this world, but be free of them.

Bhagavān Nityānanda would talk about the cashew fruit. Most seeds are inside the fruit. But the cashew nut is one seed that lives outside the fruit. So he said, "Live your life in the world in this manner." You are part of the fruit, part of the world, yet separate from it. There is a sense of detachment, yet also a sense of freedom.

Someone shared with me yesterday that she tried to invite friends to come to satsaṅg. They were a little bit worried and said, "Is he going to stare into our eyes? Is he going to do *kuṇḍalinī* movements?"

This is what people think of these days in the name of yoga. In their minds, yoga has nothing to do with contemplating "who am I?" It has nothing to do with what's going on within oneself.

Yoga has become externalized. We think that what is outside represents the path of yoga, of spirituality.

Actually, yoga has nothing to do with any of that. Yoga is about becoming free of all of those things. It is about finding steadiness. It is about finding the sense of comfort within.

Yoga is not about acting holy but about feeling holiness within yourself.

So be noble, be wise, be holy. And lead a simple life.

Eventually, hopefully, you'll become an uplifted being, an enlightened sage. But until then, at least think about these things, remember these things. Remind yourself constantly: be noble, be uplifted, be wise.

Being wise, I always say, is not about being clever. It's not about playing mind games with one another. The scriptures tell us that when one is wise, humility follows naturally. That wisdom is awake, is alive, within that person. So live in this way.

WHICH IS REAL?

Somebody asked Baba Muktānanda, "If I receive a message in a dream, how true is it?"

His answer was that the dream is as true as your waking state.

So the next question should be "How am I in my waking state?" Thinking about your waking state, ask yourself, "Am I a good person? Do I have good thoughts? Do I do good things? Are my actions uplifting?"

After you have answered those questions, understand that what happens in the dream state is a reflection of how you have been in your waking state. If you've been a good, wonderful person in your waking state, then in your dream state, wonderful things will happen to you.

The sages say the waking state is as unreal as the dream state. The dream state is as unreal as the waking state. And the deep sleep state, which many of us experience without dreams, is just as unreal.

Why is the waking state unreal?

Because as soon as I close my eyes, none of this exists for me.

Why is the dream state unreal?

Because when my eyes are closed, I am watching that dream, but when I open my eyes, I see that the dream is unreal. As much as all of this here in this room exists for me now with my eyes open, as soon as my senses withdraw into themselves, all of this becomes unreal. And whatever dream I'm having, that dream becomes unreal when I wake up.

Of course, when I get close to deep sleep, none of this exists—neither the waking nor the dream state. I'm lost, unconsciousness. The mind has become as quiet as it can. In that state of deep sleep, we come closest to the Consciousness that dwells within us.

So, in your waking state, use your time to do something that's uplifting. Do japa, repetition of the mantra. Study the scriptures. Have uplifting conversations. Do things that are beneficial.

Then, when you go into the dream state, you take these things with you into that state. The dream state is nothing but an expression of that which you perform in the waking state.

In Vedānta there is a story about King Janaka.

Janaka is fast asleep in his bed in his palace. While he is asleep, he has a dream that he goes to war with another king. He loses the war. He's tired, he's hungry. So he goes to a farm and takes some sugarcane. He begins to eat it.

The farmer comes. He tries to drive Janaka away from the field, saying, "Get out! Go away! This is my field. This is my sugarcane."

As he's being driven away, Janaka wakes up. He finds himself lying in his bed. He's in his palace. He's next to his queen.

Then he closes his eyes again. He's back in that sugarcane field. He's lost his kingdom. He's tired, he's hungry.

When he wakes up the next morning, he calls his ministers. He says, "I have a question. Which one is real: me sleeping in the bed, with my queen, in my palace, or me with eyes closed, dreaming that I've lost my kingdom and I'm being driven away by the farmer?"

Nobody has the answer to this question, so the king says, "Tomorrow I want the answer. If you don't have the answer, I'll throw you in jail!"

News begins to spread around the kingdom that King Janaka has a question none of his wise people are able to answer.

The next day, when the court gathers, a young man walks in. His name is Aṣṭāvakra. His body is bent in eight places. You can imagine that it's an odd sight.

Aṣṭāvakra walks into the court and announces to the king, "I can answer your question."

The whole court begins to laugh. The king begins to laugh. As Aṣṭāvakra watches the court laughing and the king laughing, he too begins to laugh.

When he begins to laugh, everybody else becomes quiet.

They think they know why they are laughing, but they don't know why he is laughing. What does he find so funny?

As Aṣṭāvakra walks toward him, the king asks, "O sage, why did you laugh?"

He says, "O king, first tell me why you and all your courtiers, your wise people, laughed."

The king says, "That's obvious. Look at you. Your body is bent. It looks funny, it looks strange. All these people here are considered to be the wise people of this kingdom. I have a question they were not able to answer. Yet you claim you can answer my question. But you look so funny!"

Aṣṭāvakra says, "O king, I was told that King Janaka is wise. He has satsaṅg. He's surrounded by wise people. So when I came to this court, I expected the people here to be full of wisdom. But when you began laughing, I realized you were laughing at this body. So you can't really be wise. Because all you are looking at is the external, the outside. You're not looking at what I carry within me. So therefore I laughed. I realized nobody here is as wise as I thought they would be."

Then Aṣṭāvakra addresses the king's question: which is real, the waking state in which the king is with his queen in the palace bed, or the dream in which he is in the field, eating sugarcane, having lost his kingdom, and is driven away by the farmer? He says, "O king, neither is real! Your waking state, where you are King Janaka, in your bed, with your queen, in the palace, is not real. And neither is your dream of being driven away by the farmer, as you are tired and hungry, trying to get some sugarcane to eat."

He says, "O king, what is real is the experience of the Ātman, the experience of the Self."

This is the foundation of the philosophy of Vedānta, which takes twelve, fifteen, twenty-four years to know and to understand.

In the beginning, the Guru tells us, "You are the Absolute."

And we say, "Wow! Wonderful!"

But then, in order to fully realize "I am none of this," we

do yoga. We have satsaṅg. We study, we meditate. We tell ourselves, "I am the Absolute." It is a journey that each one of us goes through. It is not the destination. It is not the goal. It is not where we want to arrive at. It is only the journey.

When we do arrive, having had glimpses along the way of oneness with Consciousness, we realize we were caught up in the game, busy in the play, the drama. Even after we have heard about the Truth and read about the Truth and understood the Truth, to actually become free of the whole play takes a long time.

BABA'S MESSAGE

I was fortunate to have met Baba Muktānanda at birth. My parents were devotees, so I lived for the first fifteen years going to the ashram on big weekends and vacations, and spending as much time as possible in Baba's company.

My parents always said, "Believe in the Guru! Trust the Guru! Love the Guru! Do what he says!"

But then I had friends in school in Mumbai who thought, "What does this boy do every weekend? Go to the ashram?"

In retrospect, I look back at all the wisdom, all the knowledge, that I sat and listened to. At times I wondered, "What is oneness? What is the Self? What is Consciousness? What is meditation?"

But then slowly I came to understand and experience and feel that which the scriptures, the sages, and the Gurus talk about. I realized it's not just a fleeting moment, it's not a glimpse here and there. We actually have to become, as Patañjali says, established in Truth, steady in Truth.

I think of the dialogue between Yājñavalkya and his young wife, Maitreyī.

He says, "We don't love each other, we don't care for each other, for the sake of each other but because of the existence of that Consciousness which is within one another."

In the Indian tradition, when somebody dies, if the death has happened early enough in the day, by sunset the body is already gone. We don't have funeral homes yet, so we don't have ways to keep the body. If the death was an accident or a murder, the matter goes to the police. Otherwise, if the death occurred at home, the doctor comes, he gives a certificate, and the body is cremated. All that is left the next day is a pot of ashes.

When someone has died, the sage asks us, "What is it that has died?"

The living physical body, the body made of five elements, is inhabited by Consciousness, by the Self, or soul as it's sometimes called in English. As soon as Consciousness has departed from that body, no matter how much we love it, we are done with that body.

I think recognizing what happens when somebody dies is the best way to understand what Yājñavalkya means when he says, "We love each other because of the existence of Consciousness."

He says, "O Maitreyī, if there is something to be seen, it is that Self. If there is something to hear about, hear about the Self, about divinity. If there is something you want to contemplate, contemplate the Self. If there is something you want to meditate upon, meditate upon the Self."

When Baba traveled all over the world, reporters would ask him, "What is your message?"

He said, "Meditate on yourself, honor yourself, worship yourself, respect yourself, because God dwells within you as you."

And the reporters said, "Anything else?"

He said, "That's it. Just understand this much: meditate, honor, respect, worship that divinity that dwells within each and every one."

And how?

He said, "See God in each other." See that divinity, see that Truth, inside your own being, and see that same divinity, that same Truth, in all. Experience that within your own Self first. Then because you see it in yourself, you see it reflected in others.

Many people claim, "I got it! I'm there. I am established. I am steady."

I offer a test. Take a jug of cold water. At night, when such a person is fast asleep, say about two o'clock in the morning, pour that cold water on their face.

If they are established in the experience "I am the Absolute," they will say, "*Oṁ Namaḥ Śivāya*" or whatever their mantra is. Otherwise, they'll say, "Who the hell is it pouring water on me?"

When I talk about becoming steady, about becoming established in Truth, that is what Patañjali wants for us. That is what the sages want. They want us to feel comfortable in that experience within ourselves. Then even if we get cold water dumped on us at 2 a.m., we remain with the mantra, we remain with divinity.

REWIND
THE TAPE OF LIFE

With great respect and love, I welcome everyone to the Intensive here today.

Meditators always ask, "What do I do with my thoughts?"

I tell them, "At least you recognize that you have thoughts." Because many people live upon this earth never realizing, "I have thoughts." Just as water is wet and fire is hot, so too does the mind have thoughts. That is the nature of the mind.

So it's not a question of getting rid of all thoughts but rather of having uplifting thoughts, noble thoughts, thoughts that will benefit us. We want to have thoughts that will benefit everyone else as well.

When we think of peace, of quiet, of silence, we realize that what the sages want us to get rid of is not the mind but our sense of "I." In the world in which we live, the sense of "I" is a very important factor we develop throughout life. So a sage simply tells us to become bigger.

The philosophy of Shaivism talks about the three *malas*, the impurities in the life of a human being. These malas veil our perception. They prevent us from seeing the Truth.

The grossest is karma mala, which refers to the actions we perform in life.

When we lived with Baba Muktānanda, we had satsaṅg every day. At the ashram in New York, the hall where we had satsaṅg had doors that swung open and closed. We were about a thousand people in that hall.

So you can imagine, we have just finished a wonderful evening chant. You are in a state of bliss. You're a little bit spaced out as you walk out of the hall, and the person ahead of you lets go of the door. The door slams, and your fingers get caught.

Your mind tells itself, "John always wanted to do that to me. I've been watching him the last few days while we've been here at the ashram, and I know he's trying to get me!"

The mind begins this process, and somehow you end up in the serving line, right behind John. In the ashram in those days, you were served soup, salad, and bread. Soup, I think, was always the first dish. So there you are with your tray. Your mind is lost in "How do I get even? How do I get back at John?"

Here on these two-lane highways on Kauai, people are so busy going straight that they forget to look out for the person who wants to turn left. In the same way, as you have your soup on your tray, you forget to notice that the person in front of you has stopped. And that person is John of course. You bump right into him, and your soup goes all over him. It's hot, it's burning, it's boiling.

Now let's just go back; let's rewind the tape. The soup goes back in the bowl, back in the pot. You're back at the door of the hall, where all this began. You're in that spacey, happy, excited, ecstatic state. This time, the door slams and catches your finger, and you simply go, "That's karma. I must have done something, and now it is part of the package of this life."

You get some ice and put it on your finger, and you resolve the situation then and there. You don't continue it for moments, days, months, years. You simply end it there.

People ask, "If that door was destined to slam and hit me, what free will do I have?"

The free will you have is how you choose to react when you find yourself in that situation. Often it's only after the fact that we realize we could have made a different choice. The philosophy of Shaivism tells us we have a choice in the moment about how we can react when we experience karma mala. Avoiding a reaction is choice number one.

Karma mala happens for each and every one of us in life. The degree may vary, but something happens to all of us. Shaivism says that moment is where a shift can take place. In modern terms, we talk about how to "respond" rather than "react." Don't do anything. Just resolve the situation within yourself.

When somebody falls down, or something happens, we have a tendency to go to that person and say, "How are you? What happened?"

That person enjoys the attention he or she is now getting. Even if it isn't a big deal, the person feels, "I can use this opportunity to say more about what happened. I will get some nice treatment as a result." The person forgets that all this does is create more karma. Instead just say, "Thanks for asking, I'm okay."

We see this with children. A child falls down. If we don't look, the child gets up and goes back to playing again. But suppose we go to the child and say, "Oh, are you hurt?"

The child says, "Yeah! Look at this!"

The child plays along with us, and we play along with the child. The child thinks he is fooling the adult, the adult thinks he's fooling the child. This is how life goes on.

When we face karma, we think, "How did I, such a good person, end up like this?" That's how we think of ourselves, right? "I'm the perfect person God created. How did I end up in this mess?"

We have to slowly rewind the tape of life.

SOFT AS BUTTER

People often tell me, "If I knew what I did in the lifetime before, then maybe I could be a better person now."

I say, "Forget the past lifetime. Just look at this lifetime and what you have done in it."

You don't need anyone else to remind you of what you have done in this lifetime. You can't just say, "I forgot yesterday." We all remember our yesterdays. We remember the days before, the months, the years. We have lots of flashbacks. We have dreams.

We wonder, "What was that dream?"

A dream is nothing but a reflection of that which we have done in the waking state. Baba says, "Just as the waking state is real to us when we are awake, a dream is real to us when we are in the dream state." The dream state feels just as real as the waking state.

Of course, from the highest viewpoint, both are unreal. From the perspective of Consciousness, the waking and the dream state and the deep sleep state are all unreal. But as long as we are in those three states, they are real for us.

Ultimately, it's a play of the mind.

The second mala that Shaivism talks about is *ānava* mala. The mind thinks to itself, "I am incomplete."

From what I can see, most coaching classes, or self-promotion classes, these days are all about thinking, "I am able to," "I can," "It's possible." Whenever you run into a difficult situation, rather than thinking, "No, I can't do it," just tell yourself, "It's possible."

However, somewhere along the way, the human mind gets the idea "I am imperfect."

Baba would say that the biggest mistake a human can make is to think this. He would sing, "I am Consciousness. I am Bliss. I am Śiva. I am the Absolute. I am perfect. I am complete. I am whole."

I would make a distinction here. There is an ego-driven sense of perfection, and there is a non-ego-driven sense of perfection. The ego-driven conviction "I'm perfect" is pushy.

You have to reconfirm it to yourself and to others. And it hurts sometimes. Because you aren't really sure if you're quite so perfect.

But when it's Consciousness-driven, it is the sense of "I am Perfect." Then it has the softness of butter. Tukārām Mahārāj describes it as butter, but he also says it is as strong as a diamond.

In society, we see people we think we would like to be like, because they seem successful in the external world. But along with that success comes a hardness. But then think of the great sage who dwells in the experience "I am the Self." There is a softness, a gentleness, a joy. We experience that softness when we chant, when we meditate, when we are in that inner space.

That experience, I always feel, is beyond words. We feel it, we experience it, we know it. But then somebody asks, "Can you describe what you feel?" And we have no words. A word is simply a word, and a word can only go so far.

THE SALT DOLL

Jñāneśvar Mahārāj tells us a doll made of salt goes to the ocean to find out how deep it is. What happens?

It dissolves.

We think to ourselves, "I want to see, I want to know, I want to experience Consciousness." When we come to that place of Consciousness, the sense of "I"—of ego, of separation, of duality—must dissolve. There is no one left to come to back and say what that experience was like.

The third mala, *māyīya* mala, is the sense "I am separate."

When each of us sits today, all we want to do is to go into the ocean of Consciousness and dissolve. We want to be free of māyīya mala.

You don't have to worry about all the basic functions. That's the question many people ask: "If I dissolve, how will life continue?"

Baba would say, "Dissolve first, and then you can worry about that."

People ask, "If I get liberated, what do I do about my life?"

I tell them, "Okay, what happens when you die? Life goes on for others. Nobody stops, nobody pauses, except maybe for a day or a few days. But then you become a memory. Life goes on. So in the higher sense, it's the same: life will continue for you and continue for others."

Baba said, "Through intense, deep meditation, you reach a state that is beyond thought, beyond change, beyond imagination, beyond differences, and beyond duality. Once you can stay in that state for a while, and can come out of it without losing any of it, then the inner divine love will begin to pour through you. You will not see people as different, as separate individuals. You will see your own Self in everyone around you."

Each of us, in our meditation, can reach that state beyond thought, beyond imagination, beyond change, beyond differences, beyond duality. But to come out of it and not lose any of it? I think that is the challenge.

The philosophy of Shaivism tells us this whole world is a

stage upon which all of us are actors. So we begin to think and see and look: Who am I in the morning, when I'm at home getting ready? Who am I as I'm driving to work? Who am I when I'm at work? Who am I at happy hour? Who am I with friends? Who am I at dinner? Who am I when I go to sleep? Am I the same from the time I wake up and all through the day or are there shifts and changes? Are there movements?

As seekers, we want to become aware: Why do I feel wonderful at times? Why am I miserable at times? Why am I anxious at times? Why am I a fanatic at times? Why…?

We put on all of these different roles and masks. Why can't we simply be steady?

This is the contemplation you need to do. Constantly ask yourself, "How can I remain steady? How can I remain stable? How can I remain in equilibrium and not allow things to affect me?"

Vedānta talks about duality. In life, we have that which gives us pleasure. And if we think about that which gives us pleasure, then the opposite is there ready to give us pain. If we get caught in deriving pleasure, then pain exists.

Brahmānanda Mahārājji used to explain that we have teeth. When we use them to eat an apple, they give us pleasure. We go to the dentist and we get them cleaned. If somebody comes to punch us in the face, we protect ourselves and say, "No, no, no, I need my teeth to eat my apple! It's giving me pleasure!"

Time goes by in life. One day you go to the dentist and pay him to remove your tooth. Because now it's hurting, it's giving you pain. Before, somebody offered to punch it out for free, and you said, "No, no, no!" But some years later in life, you go to the dentist and say, "Please remove this tooth, it's no longer giving me pleasure."

It is said, "The attachment to one thing causes an automatic aversion to something else."

When Baba talked about his Guru, Bhagavān Nityānanda, he said, "He loved nobody, but he loved everybody." Every time I heard that, it dazzled my mind. I thought, "Wow!" Because, in a way, when you first hear it, it's a contradiction. How can you love nobody and yet love everybody?

That is where the mind has to go so that it doesn't get caught in "I like, and therefore I don't like," and "I love, and therefore I don't love," and "I have pleasure, and therefore automatically I don't have pleasure," and "I'm attracted to, and so therefore automatically there is an aversion."

How do we bring about stability in the mind so it doesn't do that?

Baba said, "Be as deep as the ocean. Be as steady as a mountain." Become established in wisdom, in knowledge, in the indestructible treasure of the teachings. The mind has to be constantly centered in supreme Consciousness. Never lose courage.

The sages instruct us to use the teachings, to apply the teachings, to benefit from the teachings. Don't become a coward and say, "No! I'm going to forget the teachings for now. Right now, I'll just be *me*."

Nor do you need to constantly tell everyone, "I am established in supreme Consciousness! It's from this place of supreme Consciousness that I am telling you so!" The *Upaniṣads* say that if you have to put your knowledge on display like that, know that you don't know anything.

NOT THE DOER

Bhagavān Nityānanda sat quietly in Ganeshpuri for the last thirty-some years of his life. Thousands came to see him, yet he almost never said a word. I ask myself: what did they get in his presence? He didn't give you anything, and you didn't take anything. Yet, in that non-knowing, non-saying, nothing happening, so much happened.

The *Bhagavad Gītā* says, "I am not the doer."

We hear that and we say, "Okay, I'm not the doer!" But it doesn't work that way, because you are still thinking, "I (the doer) am not the doer." Think about it. It's just playing with your own mind. It's a play of the three malas, those veils. If you are not doing, you are not doing, so why do you have to tell yourself that you are not doing?

I met a sādhu in Mumbai. When he found out I'm from the lineage of Bhagavān Nityānanda, he asked, "Did you meet him?"

I said, "No."

He said, "Let me tell you a story. I went to Ganeshpuri in the 1950s. I'd heard a great sage was living there. When I arrived, there was a long line for darśan. Looking ahead, I could see this man lying down, facing the wall."

He said, "I paused and I said to myself, 'Why would I want to see the back of somebody?'" He meant that he wanted a proper greeting, a real recognition. When people go to meet a great sage, they expect the great sage to welcome them with open arms, to say, "O dear one, I have been waiting for you!"

The sādhu said, "But I thought, 'So many thousands come here, and I've heard of him, why don't I just go with the flow?' So I stood in line, I went up. And just as I got to him, he turned. Our eyes met. I was elated that my wish had been fulfilled."

He said, "Then I walked away, and my mind thought, 'Maybe he just turned because he was tired of lying the other way.' But I turned to look, and he was already facing the wall again. So I thought, 'Maybe he is a great sage.'"

In the Indian tradition, *darśan* literally means "to see." In Baba's time, people saw a man with peacock feathers; they saw him giving talks, meeting people. Or in the case of Bhagavān Nityānanda, they saw a man not doing anything, just lying there, or sitting or walking.

We have to think about what we really want to see. Darśan is not about the man, it's not about the human, it's not about the person. Darśan is about seeing Consciousness. It is not something seen by the physical eyes or any of the senses, but something we feel within.

When you think of last night in the temple, you might say the chanting was wonderful. You might say the space was wonderful. You might say the statue of Bhagavān was wonderful. But what happens on the physical level is not as important as what happens in the deeper level within us. All of us were together in that same vibrating Consciousness. At least for that period of time, we were inside that cave.

So as we sit here, allow yourself to be quiet, to be still, to become steady, to ponder, "What brings me here? What do I want out of this day?" Don't let it be just at a superficial, intellectual level; let it be a direct experience that you feel, that is real, that's palpable, that's true. And not because somebody else in the room said it, and therefore you agree with it—that's indirect knowledge, inference. Let it become your own direct experience, so that no matter who does what or says what, you are deep like the ocean, steady like a mountain, because you have had your own experience of Consciousness.

DISCIPLINE AND DEDICATION

With great respect and love, I welcome everyone to the Intensive here this morning. How many of you know what our topic is today? *Sādhaka, sādhanā, sādhya*. It's a personal favorite of mine because if you are here, you are the topic today. Each one of us is the topic.

A sādhaka is a seeker. Sādhanā is the practice that seeker does. And sādhya refers to the possibilities, to that which can be attained.

As I think about this, the first word that comes to mind is *discipline*. Often as I travel, people ask, "Can I do a little bit of everything?"

I tell them, "Go and ask your wife, 'Can I do a little bit of ...?' She will have a very clear answer for that."

Similarly, when people come to the Guru, they ask, "Can I do a little bit of you, and a little bit of this, a little bit of that?" The question that arises is basically about commitment: "How committed am I to the path, to the practices?"

The next word that comes to mind is *dedication*. This is an internal process. As a sādhaka, we must follow discipline, we must have dedication. Society today encourages us to think, "Hey! I'm a free individual. Why should I listen to you? Who are you to tell me what I should do?" But our scriptures tell us differently.

I'll share a story. A bunch of frogs live in a pond. At one end of the pond, there is a pole. So the frogs get together and decide to climb the pole. They all have opinions about how to do it. And they all give it a try. They go up, and they fall down. They go up, and they fall down. Only one frog makes it to the top.

The question is, why did that frog make it to the top?

"He listened to no one," the storyteller says. "He made it to the top because he did not listen to anyone."

And why did he not listen to anyone? Because he was deaf. He didn't hear all the nonsense coming from the outside world. Amazing, isn't it?

Sādhanā involves unlearning much of what the mind has been trained to think. The teaching the Guru would give to the sādhaka who wants to retrain the mind is constant practice and awareness. This means becoming simple, not complicated. But to be simple is not that simple.

Those of us in my generation and older used to get ballpoint pens, and we'd click them on and off. Inside there was a spring. In school, when we got bored with what the teacher was saying, we'd play with the spring.

Swami Brahmānandaji Mahārāj, who gave us monkhood, used to refer to the example of a spring. He said, "You keep pulling the spring. And when you let it go, it goes back to its coiled state. As a seeker, what you want to do is pull the spring so many times that it becomes a straight wire. Only after years of constant practice does the spring stay straight and not go back to its original, coiled form."

THE FOUR MEANS

Swami Śivānanda was a doctor. As a young man, he worked in British Malaysia, treating poor patients, but eventually the desire for a more spiritual kind of healing led him back to India. He ended up in Rishikesh, where he became a monk and later started the Divine Life Society. He passed away in 1963, the year after I was born. He says, "You cannot stitch without a needle and a thread. You cannot dig without a shovel or a pick. In the same way, without the four means, you cannot attain the knowledge of the Absolute."

He reminds us that a sādhaka must possess the four means of liberation described by Vedānta: viveka, *vairagya, ṣaḍsampat*, and *mumukṣutva*. That is, discrimination, dispassion, the six virtues, and a yearning for liberation.

Viveka is the ability to differentiate, or discriminate, between what is real and what is unreal.

Vairagya is not about the dispassion of going to the Himalayas or going into a forest or living in a tepee or a tent; it's about living in society, but with a sense of dispassion. Somebody says you're a wonderful person, and you're happy. Somebody says the exact opposite, and the very next moment when you turn around, you're still happy. That's dispassion.

But what happens instead? Someone walks around the ashram and says, "Did you like the food today? I was the cook. I didn't really do anything, I was just the cook." Then that person comes to me and says, "Everybody loved the food."

I say, "How do you know that?"

"Well, as I walked around, they told me how much they loved it."

The person left out one little detail. If you tell everybody you were the cook, what are they going to say? "It was horrible?" No. They'll say, "Ah, I've never had such delicious food," even if that's a lie. One thing I've learned over the years is that nobody wants to be in anybody's bad books. So we put forth all our effort to trap ourselves, to trap others.

The third means of liberation is ṣaḍsampat, the six virtues.

The first is *śama*, peace of mind. We could say it is equanimity of mind as a result of the eradication of stored impressions, desires.

Dama is control of the sense organs. The senses always want, want, want. They are never satisfied, no matter how much we give them.

Uparati is satiety, being satisfied. We simply renounce getting caught up in the act of doing. But not in the wrong way, as I just mentioned, where people sometimes say, "I'm not doing anything," even when they are very much the doers.

Titiksha is fortitude, forbearance.

Śraddhā is faith without question or without doubt. In English, we could say faith that is implicit but with wisdom, with understanding. All the checking has been done, all the questioning has been done, and we've come to a place of total, implicit faith.

Which brings us to *samādhāna*, the focus of mind that gives us complete satisfaction. How often can we claim that in life? How often are we satiated, with no want or desire for something else?

In the Indian tradition, we speak about the path of *dharma*. Dharma means that which is right, that which is correct, that which feels complete to the individual. His or her duty. A seeker who follows dharma is disciplined. His life is about austerity, about simplicity. His nature is steadfastness. Because he follows the right path, he is steady in his mind, he speaks the truth.

We say we speak the truth, but we know within ourselves how much truth we actually speak. It's not truth simply because we say, "I'm going to say the truth!" Truth has to be that which, when heard, is also pleasing and beneficial. Otherwise keep quiet. Don't say, "I'm speaking the truth and I don't care what you feel!" The scriptures say don't speak like that. Those words don't have the desired effect, even if they are the so-called truth.

To do good actions, you don't have to inspire yourself by saying to yourself, "I'll be good today." It should be a natural outcome.

I hope you remember all this.

If we examine what Swami Śivānanda is telling us, we see that a lot of conditions are being placed on a seeker whose claim is "I'm doing my spiritual practice."

You can't just say, "I'm going to meditate away all my problems." When you come out of meditation sixty minutes later, the problems will still be just as much there. If not worse, because now you are aware of them. Sixty minutes before, you at least weren't aware of them, because you were a happy-go-lucky person.

A seeker makes the decision to do his or her practices, and through that sādhanā, to reach sādhya, the possibilities that can be attained.

The first is easy—to be a seeker. The second is also easy—to do the practices. But the third, sādhya, is more difficult. Because the possibilities to be attained are infinite. Of course, from the scriptural point of view, the possibilities are defined specifically as knowledge of the Absolute, knowledge of the Truth, the experience of the Divine. Yet think how vast that experience can be.

THE SIXTY QUALITIES

Swami Śivānanda's books are straight to the point. Either you do spiritual practices, or you get out of the way. I found many of his thoughts compiled in one place, where he lists sixty qualities of a seeker. When you read them, you think, "Oh! I can do this!" Let's go through them.

First, he says, reduce your wants to the utmost minimum.

Adapt yourself to circumstances.

Never be attached to anything or anybody.

Share what you have with others.

Be ever ready to serve, lose no opportunity. Don't say, "Do you want me to give you a hand?" or "How can I give you a hand?" or "Where do you want me to give you a hand?" That means you never wanted to give your hand, because you are asking so many questions. At the same time, Swami Śivānanda says, entertain non-doership. In Swamiji's mind, the seeker is saying, "Who am I to give you a hand, when there is nobody here to give a hand?"

Be a witness. Simply observe. Just do what needs to be done, don't get caught in it—like in the example I gave earlier: "Did you like my food?" or "Didn't I do a good job?"

Speak measured and sweet words. A wife goes to the sage and says, "Every night when my husband comes home, we have a fight, we argue." The sage gives her some holy water and says, "Every time your husband comes home, put this in your mouth." A month later, she comes back to the sage. She says, "I need some more holy water." He says, "How is everything?" She says, "Wonderful. But I need more holy water. Because every day when my husband comes home, I need to put it in my mouth." The sage says, "No. Just control your tongue. That's all you need to do."

Have a burning thirst for God-realization. That is the fourth means described by Vedānta: mumukṣutva. That yearning should always be there.

Renounce all your belongings and surrender yourself to God. That doesn't mean you should pack up and come here to the ashram, or go someplace else. Just take a look at what you could renounce that is inside your closet, inside your pantry, inside your garage, in storage. Thanksgiving is coming, Christmas is coming. Go to a landfill. Go to the Salvation Army. Go to all the places where people bring things they feel they don't need anymore. Look in trash cans. See how much stuff we throw away. When Swamiji says to renounce all your belongings and surrender yourself to God, he means to feel your connection to divinity, so that you can learn how not to accumulate what's unnecessary.

The spiritual path is a sharp-edged razor path. A Guru is absolutely necessary. So just stay on the path, keep at it. You need guidance, you need somebody who can help you.

Have great patience and perseverance. Accept the circumstances, accept the situation, accept what is in life. And have patience. The circumstances will change, but it will take time. Not today, not tomorrow. The change has to be within you. We always think the change has to be out there. No, the change has to be in us.

Never leave your practice, even for a day. I always say that the day you miss it, the day you feel "I don't want to do it," is the day you need to do it. Because if you don't do it today, tomorrow you will tell yourself, "It was okay yesterday, it worked out." Before you know it, it's been a few months since you did the practice.

The Guru will only guide you; you yourself must tread the path. Swamiji says something very important here: the practice has to be done by you. Don't think, "I'll just bow to the Guru, and a miracle will happen." If that worked, why wouldn't we do it at mealtimes? When it's lunchtime, you could sit here and say, "Baba will take care of my thirst, Baba will take care of my stomach." No, you have to walk all the way down to Namaste; you have to make sure you're the first one in line for the meal.

Life is short. The time of death is uncertain. So apply yourself seriously to the practice, to sādhanā.

Maintain a daily spiritual diary. Correctly record your progress and failures. Stick to your resolve.

Don't complain that there is no time for sādhanā. Reduce your talk. Reduce your sleep. Meditate during the auspicious early morning hours, two to three hours before sunrise. Waking up early means you have to go to bed early. Here, we go to bed early and we wake up early.

Let the thought of God keep away thoughts of the world. Keep your mind focused on divinity, so it stays away from everything else.

Forget the thought "I am a woman" or "I am a man." Swamiji says your contemplation of the divine should be vigorous.

Never postpone a thing for tomorrow if it is possible for you to do it today. Make your bed every morning. I go to so many homes where the beds are not made. In the Indian tradition, when we slept on a mattress, we were told to roll it up in the morning. They said that was so negativity didn't come and live in that mattress during the day.

Don't boast or make a show of your abilities. Be simple and humble.

Always be cheerful. Give up worries.

Be indifferent to things that don't concern you.

Fly away from discussion and company.

Be alone for a few hours daily. These days, that is difficult.

Give up being greedy, being jealous, and hoarding. Again, difficult in our society. Greed is what has brought our society to where it is today.

Control your emotions through discrimination and dispassion.

Maintain equilibrium of mind always.

Think twice before you speak and thrice before you act.

Give up backbiting, criticizing, and fault finding. Beware of your reactions.

We all have reactions. Instead acting blindly on them, find your own faults and weaknesses. See only good in others, praise their virtues.

Forgive and forget the harm done by others. Do good to those who hate you. When I read this, I thought, "Oh, I have to make sure I stress this." So I am: forgive and forget the harm.

That's difficult in itself, but then Swamiji says, "Do good to those who hate you."

Shun lust, anger, egoism, delusion, greed. How? As you would avoid a venomous cobra. I think this should be taught in school—in kindergarten, in first grade, in second grade, as the child is growing up—not when we are already thirty, forty, fifty. Then, by the time the child is a teenager or a young person, these are natural instincts within the human being.

Swamiji says an interesting thing here: be prepared to suffer any amount of pain. I won't comment on this, because I have my own thoughts about that. How much is any amount? We'd have to read his books to really understand what he means by this statement.

Always have a set of maxims with you to induce dispassion.

Treat sensual enjoyment as poison, vomited food, or urine. The mind should always be immersed in the thought of the Absolute; that's how you take it away from the pleasures of the senses. Coming from Malaysia, where he was a doctor, Swamiji probably experienced having everything life could give him. Yet there he was in Rishikesh, so at some point, he must have thought of all these things for himself.

Preserve your semen carefully. Always sleep separately.

Revere women as Mother Divine. Imagine if a child learned this while young. We wouldn't have so many of the issues we have today. When people look at someone, that someone is simply a sex object. Instead, we want to see that person is nothing but an expression of the Divine.

See God in every face, in everything.

Take to chanting, satsaṅg, or prayer whenever the mind is overpowered by base instincts.

Face obstacles coolly and boldly. Be bold. Be courageous.

When you are on the right path, care not for criticism, yield not to flattery. Just do what needs to be done and don't care about either praise or blame.

Respect rogues and scoundrels. Serve them. Again, we'll have to read more by Swamiji to fully understand this.

Admit your faults plainly.

Take care of your health. Do not neglect daily āsana and exercise.

Be active and nimble, always.

Develop your heart by giving. Be extraordinarily charitable. Give more than what you expect to receive.

Desires multiply misery. Develop contentment.

Control the senses, one by one.

Develop *brahmākāra vṛtti*. Swamiji uses a technical term here, referring to thoughts that have taken the shape of the Divine. *Akāra* is form or shape; *vṛtti* is the thought modifications of the mind. So Vedānta says brahmākāra vṛtti is the final state of the mind before it merges into the Absolute, at which point there is no mind left, and the limited self is now experiencing liberation.

Keep a check on all your thoughts. Keep them pure and sublime.

Don't lose your temper when anyone insults, taunts, or rebukes you. Hear it as a mere play of words or a variety of sounds. Just think that they're off-key.

Rest your mind in God, and live in Truth.

Get up and keep following the path of perfection.

Have a definite aim in your life, and proceed cautiously. That's something our society needs today. What is your goal, your destination? Know that and keep going toward it.

The benefits of silence are incalculable. Observe silence, beginning with at least one hour a day. And it shouldn't be when you're sitting to meditate or doing another of your practices.

Four important means that allow passion to enter the mind are sound, touch, sight, and thoughts. Be vigilant when it comes to what you see, what you hear, what you touch, and of course what is going on inside your own mind.

Have an intimate connection with no one but God. Mix little with others.

Be moderate in everything; extremes are dangerous.

Do self-analysis and introspection every day.

So, how many of you can remember all of these qualities that Swami Śivānanda describes? That was fifty-nine. If you take some of these qualities and start applying them every day, over time you will see a shift, a change.

The last quality is to give up curiosities on the spiritual path. Conserve your energy and concentrate. Think little of food, of the body, and your relatives. Think more of the Self. You must realize the Self in this very birth.

What Swamiji is saying is, if you do all of the above, the outcome will be the experience of the Self, of the Ātman.

I think these are all qualities we need before we even begin the journey. So for those who think you've already begun, maybe take a closer look. Of course, you can fake it to yourself and say, "I have at least fifty-five of them." But then we'll throw you in the washing machine, and that will tell us how established you really are in all these qualities.

THERE IS NOTHING THAT IS NOT CONSCIOUSNESS

So how do we get to our destination?

First, the seeker has all of his sixty qualities. I think it's actually more than sixty, because sometimes Swami Śivānanda included so many within one. Then the seeker asks, "What is it that I must do? And as the seeker is doing his sādhanā, he asks, "Where is it that I must arrive?"

You can think of the ocean. When you stand on the shore, looking at the ocean, the ocean has many waves. You get excited—especially if you're a surfer—at the ten-foot, twelve-foot, fifteen-foot waves. You forget that each wave is nothing but the ocean.

There is no separation or difference created when the ocean becomes a wave. The wave comes from the ocean, it forms a wave, and then it falls back into the ocean.

It is the same with us. Within the ocean of Consciousness, all the various forms of the world arise as waves. Seeing this, the poet-saint Dharmadās asks, "Is there really any coming and going?" The truth, he says, is that there is nothing that is not Consciousness. Whatever exists is complete. It is all Consciousness. Everything simply comes to rest in the Self.

The next time you go to the beach, absorb this teaching. The ocean arises, it becomes a wave, and that wave merges back into the ocean. As you watch the ocean and have that vision, you realize that all these forms—all the people, all of creation—are nothing but waves in the ocean.

GLOSSARY

Abhinavagupta: [993-1015] Shaivite sage
āchārya: teacher
Ādi Śaṅkarācārya: [788-820] sage, originator of Advaita Vedānta
ahaṁ Brahmāsmi: mantra meaning "I am the Absolute"
āhāra: food
ahiṁsā: nonviolence
akāra: form, shape
Akbar: [1542-1605] Moghul emperor in India
ama: toxic waste from digestion, causes disease
ānanda: bliss
Annakuṭa: Hindu festival; literally, mountain of food
aparigraha: non-acquisitiveness
āratī: waving of lights to worship a deity
Arjuna: a warrior, hero of the *Bhagavad Gītā*
āsana: yogic posture
aṣṭāṅga yoga: eight-limbed yoga described by Patañjali
Aṣṭāvakra: a Vedic sage
Aṣṭāvakra Gītā: Hindu scripture
asteya: non-covetousness
Ātman: the soul, Self
avadhūta: one who has gone beyond body consciousness
Avadhūta Stotram: verses about the qualities of a sage
āyāma: expansion
Āyurveda: the ancient Indian science of health
Bhagavad Gītā: Hindu scripture
bhanḍārā: feast
Birbal: King Akbar's prime minister
brahmacharya: celibacy
brahmākāra: shape of the divine
Brahman: the Absolute
Brahmānanda: [1772-1832] poet-saint
buddhi: intellect
Bulleh Shah: [1680-1758] Punjabi Islamic poet
Caitra: March/April
Cāndogya Upaniṣad: scripture from *Sāma Veda*

Chandi Pāṭha: Sanskrit mantras to the Goddess
Chinmayānanda, Swami: [1916–1993], wrote a commentary on the *Bhagavad Gītā*
Chokhamela: [14th c.] poet-saint of Maharashtra
dama: controlling the senses
darśan: vision of the divine, experienced in the presence of a holy being
Dhairyalakṣmī: the Goddess of patience and fortitude
Dhanalakṣmī: the Goddess of wealth
Dhanyalakṣmī: the Goddess of grains
dhāraṇā: concentration
dharma: right action, righteous law
Dharmadās: [15th c.] poet-saint, disciple of Kabīr
dhyāna: meditation
Dīpāvalī: Hindu festival of lights
dṛṣṭi: vision
Eknāth Mahārāj: [1528-1609] saint
Gajālakṣmī: the elephant Goddess
Gaṇeśa: elephant-headed god, son of Śiva, remover of obstacles
Guru Gītā: commentary on the Guru
gurukula: school of the Guru
Guru Pūrṇimā: full moon of the Guru in July
Haṁsa: mantra; literally, "I am That"
hiṁsā: cruelty, harm
icchā-śakti: power of will
Indra: Lord of Heaven
Janaka, King: Vedic king, student of Aṣṭāvakra
japa: repetition of a mantra
Jayalakṣmī: the Goddess of victory
jñāna: knowledge
Jñāneśvar Mahārāj: [13th c.] poet-saint of Maharashtra
Kabīr: [1440-1518] poet-saint and weaver
Kali Yuga: the dark age, the last of four ages
karmakand: rituals

Kashmir Shaivism: philosophy based on the idea that all is Consciousness

Kaṭha Upaniṣad: a scripture

kirtan: chanting

kriyā-śakti: the power to make manifest

Kṛṣṇa: Hindu deity, Guru of Arjuna in the *Bhagavad Gītā*

kuṇḍalinī: spiritual energy dormant within all humans, can be awakened by the Guru

laddu: ball-shaped Indian sweet

Lakṣmī: the Goddess of abundance

Lalitā Sahasranāma: chant of the thousand names of the Goddess

liṅgam: form of the formless Śiva

Magod: village in Gujarat, India, where a Shanti Mandir ashram is located

Mahākālī: the great Goddess who removes ignorance

Mahālakṣmī: the great Goddess of abundance

mahāsamādhi: final merging with the Absolute

Mahāsarasvatī: the great Goddess of knowledge

Maitreyī: wife of Yājñāvalkya

mala: one of three veils, or impurities (ānava, māyīya, karma)

mālā: a string of beads used like a rosary

mantra: sacred words or syllables, literally "that which protects the mind"

Mehta, Narsinh: [15th c] Gujarati poet-saint

Mīrābāī: [1498-1547] poet saint and queen

mumukṣutva: longing for liberation

Muṇḍaka Upaniṣad: a scripture

Nāciketa: boy hero of Kaṭha Upaniṣad

namaḥ: salutations

namaste: I offer my salutations to the divine within you

Nārada: divine sage

Nārāyaṇa: Lord Viṣṇu, God of sustenance

Nasruddin, Mullah: Sufi folk character

Navarātra: nine-night celebration of the Goddess

nasya: related to the nose

nityabodha: self-illuminating
niyama: restraint
nitya: eternal
Oṁ: primordial sound
Oṁ Namaḥ Śivāya: mantra; literally, "I bow to the divine within"
Oṁ Namo Bhagavāte Muktānandāya: chant honoring Baba Muktānanda
pakhawaj: Indian drum
Pārvatī: Hindu goddess, wife of Śiva
Patañjali: [2nd c BCE] author of the *Yoga Sūtras*
prāṇa: the life breath
prāṇāyāma: regulation of the breath
prārabdha: karma from a former life that is due to appear in this lifetime
prasād: blessed gift
pratyāhāra: withdrawal of the senses
puṇya: merit
pūjā: worship
rajas: the quality of passion
rājasika: having the quality of passion
Rāma/Rām: incarnation of Lord Viṣṇu
Rāmāṇa Maharṣi: [1879-1950] contemporary Indian saint
Sadguru: true Guru
sādhaka: seeker; one who does sādhanā
sādhanā: spiritual practices
sādhu: a mendicant
sādhya: possibilities; that which can be attained
ṣaḍsampat: six virtues
sahasrāra: the crown chakra (energy center)
Śakti: the Goddess
śakti: the creative energy of the universe
śaktipāt: transmission of śakti by the Guru
śama: peace of mind
samādhāna: concentration of mind
samādhi: union with the Absolute

samadṛṣṭi: equal vision
samabhāva: feeling of oneness
sanātan: universal, eternal
sandhyā: transitions, dawn and dusk
Santānalakṣmī: the Goddess who oversees the ability to have children
śarada: autumn
sarve: all
satsaṅg: in the company of the Truth
sāttva: the quality of purity
sāttvika: having a pure quality
satya: truthfulness
sevā: work offered as service to the Guru
Shaivism: philosophy based on the idea that all is Consciousness
Sharan, Hari Om: [1932-2007] devotional singer
siddha: perfected master
Sītā: Rāma's wife
Śiva: Hindu deity, the primordial Guru
Śivānanda, Swami: [1887–1963] founder of the Divine Life Society
śivāya: auspiciousness
śraddhā: faith
Śrī: used to indicate reverence
steya: stealing
śubha: auspicious, happy
śuddha: pure
sukha: pleasure, contentment
sūtra: aphorism, verse
Taittirīya Upaniṣad: Hindu scripture
tamas: the quality of darkness and inertia
tāmasika: having the quality of inertia
Tat tvam asi: You art That
titiksha: fortitude
trikāla: three times
Tukārām Mahārāj: [1608-1650] poet saint

Upaniṣads: ancient Hindu scriptures
uparati: being satiated, without worldly longings
Vaibhavalakṣmī: the Goddess of grandeur
vairagya: dispassion
vasānta: spring
Vedānta: philosophy based on the *Vedas*
Vedas: ancient Hindu scriptures
Vidyālakṣmī: the Goddess of knowledge
Vijayalakṣmī: the Goddess of victory
Vijñāna Bhairava: 7th c. Kashmir Shaivism text
Viṭṭhal: form of Lord Viṣṇu
viveka: discrimination between the real and the unreal
Vivekānanda, Swami: [1863-1902] disciple Rāmakrishna
vṛtti: modification of the mind
vyādhi: illness
yama: disciplined practice
Yājñavalkya: sage, one of the authors of the *Upaniṣads*
Yoga Sūtras: scripture compiled by Patañjali
Yoga Vāsiṣṭha: scripture narrating dialogue between Rāma and sage Vāsiṣṭha

MAHĀMANDALESHWAR SWAMI NITYĀNANDA

Mahāmandaleshwar Swami Nityānanda is from a lineage of traditional spiritual teachers in India. While carrying the traditional teachings, he makes spirituality a practical part of modern daily reality, guided by the prayer "May all beings live in peace and contentment."

Born in 1962, Swami Nityānanda was raised from birth in an environment of yoga and meditation. His parents were devotees of the famous ascetic *avadhūta* Bhagavān Nityānanda, and then became disciples of his successor, the renowned Guru Baba Muktānanda.

Swami Nityānanda was trained from childhood by Baba Muktānanda and initiated into the mysterious path of the Siddha Gurus. He learned the various yogic practices, including meditation and Sanskrit chanting, and studied the philosophies of Vedānta and Kashmir Shaivism.

He was initiated into the Sarasvatī order of monks in 1980 at eighteen years of age and was given the name Swami Nityānanda by Baba Muktānanda. In 1981, Baba Muktānanda declared Swami Nityānanda would succeed him to carry on the lineage.

In 1987, Swami Nityānanda founded Shanti Mandir as a vehicle for continuing his Guru's work and subsequently established four ashrams.

In 1995, at the age of thirty-two, at a traditional ceremony in Haridwar, India, the ācāryas and saints of the Daśnām tradition installed him as a Mahāmandaleshwar of the Mahānirvani Akhara. He is the youngest recipient since the inception of this order.

Currently Swami Nityānanda, also known as Gurudev, travels around the world, sharing the spiritual practices in which he has been trained.

Mahāmandaleshwar Swami Nityānanda

SHANTI MANDIR

Shanti Mandir, a spiritual nonprofit organization, is dedicated to the propagation of Baba Muktānanda's teachings.

One of the ashrams of Shanti Mandir is near the banks of the River Ganges, at Kankhal, near Haridwar. The ashram at Magod is in rural surroundings, amidst a twenty-acre mango orchard, in the state of Gujarat. The third ashram in India is adjacent to the samādhi shrine of Bhagavān Nityānanda, in the village of Ganeshpuri, in Maharashtra state. Shanti Mandir's ashram in the United States is on 294 wooded acres outside the town of Walden, New York.

Under the guidance of Swami Nityānanda, Shanti Mandir symbolizes peace, progress, and love. In addition to the spiritual practices carried on daily, these ashrams contribute their resources toward the following charitable activities: Śrī Muktānanda Sanskrit Mahāvidyālaya (education), Shanti Arogya Mandir (health), and Shanti Hastkala (economic upliftment through handicrafts).

Baba Muktānanda

Bhagavān Nityānanda

LOKĀḤ SAMASTĀḤ SUKHINO BHAVANTU

MAY ALL BEINGS BE CONTENT

www.ingramcontent.com/pod-product-compliance
Lightning Source LLC
Chambersburg PA
CBHW072149100526
44589CB00015B/2146
* 9 7 8 1 7 3 6 3 9 4 2 2 9 *